Gold Man Review

Gold Man Review is published once a year by Gold Man Publishing in Salem, Oregon.

Subscriptions available at www.goldmanpublishing.com

The editors invite submissions of previously unpublished works of fiction, nonfiction, and poetry. Manuscripts can be submitted at www.goldmanpublishing.com by following our submission guidelines.

Copyright 2013/2014 Gold Man Publishing / Gold Man Review LLC.
P.O. Box 8202, Salem, OR 97303
Printed by Gold Man Publishing
ISSN: 2162-8238
ISBN: 978-0-615-89895-7

Contents

Letter from the Editors

"And the day came when the risk to remain tight in a bud was more painful than the risk it took to blossom."
—Anaïs Nin

It's our third year of *Gold Man Review*, a triumph for a journal that printed its first issue with a lot of hope and an unknown future. The last three years have brought opportunities and challenges that none of us ever anticipated when we decided to pool our collective efforts and create a journal that would make our community of writers proud. Despite the dire outlook of new journals, each year that passes we dig our literary foot a little further into the ground and look forward to what the next year brings.

While we never ask specifically for themes, every year they emerge. In *Gold Man Review Issue 3*, children and childhood appears more often than not, particularly the growing pains of change and transformation. These same themes have also been felt at the heart of *Gold Man*. For the first three years, the world was new and we tentatively explored it by learning to crawl and then taking our first steps. Now, we are on the move, literally and figuratively. As *Gold Man Review* grows once more, we head into a new direction.

Gold Man Review is turning into a West Coast journal. Starting with *Issue 4*, we'll be opening submissions to not only Oregon, but to California, Washington, Hawaii, and Alaska, essentially any state that touches the Pacific. This is an exciting upcoming change for *Gold Man* and we await the possibilities that come with it. As we make this transition, we want our Oregon contributors to know that we will always be grateful that they took a chance on an unknown literary journal and helped make *Gold Man Review* what it is today. We couldn't have done this without them.

Sincerely,

Gold Man Review Editors

Editor-in-Chief
Heather Cuthbertson

Project Editor
Nicklas Roetto

Executive Editor
Marilyn Ebbs

Senior Editor
Darren Howard

Editor
Sandra McDow

Editor
Mark Russell Reed

Editor
Lois Rosen

Would You Read It?
by Don Kunz

If it didn't look like some kind of poem,
Would you read it?
When you glimpsed those words
Spreading like a coffee stain across the morning news
Or those sentences broken like legs
On a cold white page slick and treacherous as a ski slope
Or those peculiar phrases scrambling
Your thoughts into the ravings of a stroke victim
Or if it didn't look packed with ideas like 42 bozos
Ready to pour out of a VW Beetle into your center ring,
(And we're talking serious bozos, not a lot of laughs),
Would you read it?

What if you refused to call it a poem?
What if you, oh, I don't know,
Called it a screenplay maybe,
So you could think you wouldn't have to think,
Just let the words make a movie in your hungry head?
So, you could sit in the dark,
Your mouth filled with popcorn and milk duds,
And let the cold light from your eyes become a projector
Inventing the screen where you could watch
Car chases down blue-black rain-slick streets
Where steam rose from sewer grates
And dimly lit flower stores
Suddenly exploded into crackling yellow flame
And a guy in a fedora fired at you from the shadows
Beside an industrial strength dumpster
Waiting in an alley behind a fancy restaurant.
Would you read it?

And what if it looked like that other kind of poem,
Would you read it?
When you stumbled over those measured lines
Laid out like stiffs waiting for a coffin
But precisely balanced,
A playground see saw
Where end rhymes perched
Not like delighted children
    But mannequins or midgets,
      And when you stood before those stanzas,
        Cement blocks squatting square and stolid
          Rising into staircases threatening exercise,
            But you really needed an express elevator
              If you were going to get to the bottom of

Or on top of
What you now realized was one big unforgiving mother of a philosophical
skyscraper,
Would you read it?

Or would it make you want to turn suicide bomber,
A guy who could bring it all down to earth,
All down around your aching head
Stuffy with advertising jingles
And greeting cards with smiley faces
And oh-baby-oh-baby-oh-baby pop crap
Because it had already blown your mind
And you figure it's the only way to find out
What that odd architecture is made of?
If this poem fell on you like more than a ton of bricks,
Something concrete raining down from the abstract sky,
Would you feel like you had read it?

Miracle Play
—Riverfront Park, Bend, Oregon
by Paulann Petersen

At afternoon rehearsal God wore
a cowboy hat, simply talking
his way through the lines, his voice
saved for this real performance
when he climbs the platform, stage right,
to announce his presence.
Come forth to paradise, he calls
to an Adam dressed in a flesh body suit,
Eve in a shimmer
of clinging black. Geese exit
the river, ducks too,
the sun making its last breaks
through willow limbs as it wavers down
into the horizon. *Every fruit by its right name
I shall gather,* promises Adam.

A groundling child on the grass watches,
the hood of his red trick-or-treat costume
pronged with gleaming plastic horns.
Geese honk. A baby in its mother's arms
sputters, cries out. *Take this apple
in thy hand and bite,* says the player
cast as Satan. The tiny devil's sister
wears Superman pajamas, the cape
static-stuck to her back. *Woman, therefore
shall thou be underling and bear
thy child with great groaning,* an angel declaims.

The mother lifts her blouse over
the baby's head to suckle,
while another angel speaks of that meekest,

purest virgin, played by the actress with pale
permed hair and a stripe of sunburn
painting her nape: *Her body*
shall be filled with bliss.

The river, sliding, soughing,
night air pressing the cold close.
Watchers huddle, despite
what they next hear:
God's grace shall lighten thee.
Then sudden. The baby
that angel hands to Mary
is real. Pink gums, waving arms.
The audience gasps.
Out come the cameras—
bright bright bright
countless flashes of wonder
breach the dark.

Some Tigers – A Story in Two Parts
by Linda Ferguson

Part 1

Larry dresses his tiger in handmade shirts from Bali.

When Michael got drafted, he tried to take his tiger with him, but the army said the tiger might scare the enemy.

Roberto, a magician, taught his tiger how to disappear.

Harriet, a social worker, trained her tiger to take foster kids for rides on its velvet back.

Jean-Claude and his tiger like to ski.

Angelina's tiger pours real maple sugar on its buttermilk pancakes.

Marguerite's tiger mows and waters the lawn for her while she flips through a magazine.

Frank's tiger has excellent taste in furniture.

Honoré's tiger smokes dope and dozes on the couch all afternoon.

Rodrigo sent his tiger to seminary, but his tiger knows it was born to be an accountant.

Lucy's tiger generously shares its freshly caught prey with her.

Part 2

My tiger is a competitive chess player who recently sold its stamp collection on eBay.

Here's a riddle: What's five years older than me after February 4th and six years older than me after September 15th? Answer: My tiger!

My tiger and I are on speaking terms, but just barely. Sometimes we sit together, by all appearances enjoying one another's company, but I'm always prepared, ears pricked and muscles tensed, ready to leap up and run if my tiger should get a hankering to lunge.

One time I decided to be brave. It was October and we were sitting on the lawn. My tiger had just gotten some very bad news and was quiet. The pink and purple asters were in full-bloom, and the autumn sun was shining on my tiger's radiant fur. Compelled by the beauty of the day and a fragrance of lingering tenderness, I reached out to touch my tiger. It whipped its head around and tore off my index finger.

That was a long time ago, but I find such things hard to forgive. Confession: The other day my tiger, who lost its last three chess tournaments, came by and asked me for money. In response, I waved my hand—the one with the missing digit—as if to bat away a mosquito. Also, when my tiger's wife asked me to bring the appetizers for Thanksgiving dinner, I snapped, "Sorry, my manual dexterity isn't what it used to be."

Too harsh? Well, I have other stories—a bloody lip, a surprise lurking in my closet, and an incident involving my tiger's tail and a particularly vicious round of crack the whip. Here's my favorite one: On my 35th birthday, my tiger called me out of the blue. I hadn't heard from it in some time, so I was touched. But instead of singing to me, my tiger roared so fiercely my next-door neighbor heard it and ran over to see if he should call the police. "Oh," I laughed, "that was just my tiger." Afterwards, though, I felt like crying and my hand trembled that night when I tried to brush my teeth.

Only my friends with tigers would understand, which is why I tell this story to them at every opportunity. I tell Marguerite and Larry, Rodrigo and Michael. I tell Jean-Claude and Harriet and Honoré.

Roberto says his tiger can be inconsiderate too: "One time I make him disappear, and he not come back for a week." In a lowered voice, Frank says he's found fur on his blue silk Louis Quinze loveseat. Apparently that no-good tiger of Angelina's threw a tantrum one morning when she was running late and tried to serve it instant coffee.

"But your tiger is the worst," my friends agree. "That's one ferocious beast."

Only Lucy tells me differently. She's never met my tiger, but every time I tell my story she shakes her head sadly and says, "But you don't see."

"I see this!" I cry, waggling my four-fingered hand in her face, but she shakes her head again. "No, you don't see." Then I lean forward in my seat, hoping she'll say something new, that she'll finally explain the mystery. But every time she says the same thing:

"In its heart, your tiger harbors great affection for you."

Toilet Paper
by Penelope Schott
　　　for Eli when he had just turned 9

My grandson knows what's funny:

the word sponge collapses us both
into giddy laughter

because the Roman legionnaires
used to share a sea sponge on a stick

for toilet paper.

We learned this fact in England
where he and I stood together

on Hadrian's Wall

sharing sixteen centuries
with sixty years between us.

So many years

and places I won't see – who knows
where my grandson might travel?

Somewhere

bats suckle on cactus blossoms
under the moon,

and I know without seeing it
exactly how light

will shine through their wings.

There Once Was a Girl Named Maria
by Michael T. Coolen

I saw Maria for the first time when I was fifteen years old. I was walking to O'Dea Catholic High School for boys, and Maria was walking on Marion Street with some friends in the opposite direction on her way to Immaculate Catholic High School for girls. I almost stopped breathing because she was so beautiful with her golden hair and a heart-melting smile. She moved like a ballet dancer. I waved at her. Actually, I just lifted my right index finger. I was in love for the first time. Well, there was Annette Funicello earlier in my life, but that was a very immature kind of love. I was only eleven and didn't know true love.

I was so shy that I used my peripheral vision to catch a glimpse of her; so much so that sometimes I thought my eyes would get stuck permanently on the right side of my head. Week after week, we passed each other on the way to school. Although I normally walked pretty fast, when I was passing her, I cut my speed in half hoping she would say hello or need rescuing from a mugger or something. Finally, I knew I had to take drastic action, and my inspiration came from a recently released film.

In 1961, the movie version of *West Side Story* came out. I was a sophomore at O'Dea, and it seemed that everyone was excited about the movie except maybe one teacher, Brother Donnelly (a.k.a. "The Beaker" among the students because of his nose). Raised in New York, he felt it was an evil film glorifying New York gangs. The Beaker was a guy who went around saying, "Knock on wood," and then thumping some unsuspecting student on the head.

Anyway, I saw the movie version of *West Side Story* in 1961, and I loved it. Richard Beymer was the perfect Tony, and Natalie Wood was the hottest older woman named Maria I'd ever seen. I saw myself in Tony when he sang "Maria." Saying the lyrics softly makes it almost like praying. Richard Beymer was like my avatar, before there were avatars. Later in life I learned that Marlon Brando, based on his experience in the 1955 film musical *Guys and Dolls*, wanted the role of Tony. The idea of Marlon Brando mumbling "I justmetagilnameMaria" still gives me occasional gas.

As a sophomore at O'Dea it was easy to see myself as a kind of Irish Tony, and Maria as, well, Maria. My Maria was Russian, but so what? It seemed fated that she and I were destined to be together. All I had to do was perform "Maria" for her, and she would fall into my arms, pledging her undying love. How I arrived at this plan still escapes me, but I was only 15. Hormones triumphed over logic.

I decided to learn how to play "Maria" on the piano for three main reasons: First, I had already tried unsuccessfully to learn the violin from my father. I got as far as "Down By the Sea" when I was 7, but no further.

Second, I thought about walking down the side of my street playing a guitar and singing "Maria," but since my voice was still undecided between boy soprano and bullfrog, singing was definitely not an option.

Third, my family owned an old Estey upright piano. "Ergo," I thought, "piano is the logical choice." We studied a lot of Latin at O'Dea. For the Episcopalians and Buddhists reading this, "ergo" means "therefore."

There were a couple of major challenges to my plan. Lessons were not an option, since my three older sisters had used up all the parental money and patience for children's music lessons, and my parents decided the three younger boys were "on their own." Another problem was that my older brother, Dick, was a jazz and rock and roll pianist, and for years he had brought his "gang" over to play about as loud as they could in our living room, which was only slightly larger than the drum kit. The kitchen and my parents' bedroom shared adjacent walls with the living room. So by the time I wanted to learn how to play piano, the fallboard (the part of the piano that closes over the keys) had been nailed shut by my parents. They were tired of hearing "Tutti frutti" played over and over, and a little suspicious of what the lyrics really meant.

It was my mother, the hard-working nurse, who took over the task of teaching me how to play. They weren't really formal lessons; more like five minutes here and there. She helped me learn how to read notes. I didn't start by opening the pages of beginner piano books. I went right out and bought a copy of the sheet music for "Maria."

I wasn't a prodigy. But obsessive love combined with six hours of practice each day produced quick results. I learned to play "Maria" competently in a month, as long as nobody talked to me while I was playing.

Now that I had the means to win Maria's heart and soul with my fingers, so to speak, the next obstacle arose. I had to find a way to get A (Michael) and B (Maria) simultaneously in the same place as C (a piano). I prayed daily that God would miraculously provide a piano on the sidewalk just as I was passing Maria on the way to school. Maybe somebody would be moving a piano in or out of a house, and I would sit down and play for Maria as she walked by. For weeks I looked for one out of my peripheral vision, waiting for God to perform a miracle because I longed to feel Maria in my arms. I knew that, in the name of true love, God would come through for me.

God didn't. Nietzsche was right. God was dead. Or at least He was pretty inattentive. I never got to play the piano for Maria, and she later married a friend of mine named Michael. A coincidence? Hardly. I think I'd sensed there was a Michael in Maria's destiny. I was just mistaken about which Michael it was. I was devastated that I never got to play my song for her. I mean, I'm not sure the other Michael could even spell piano, much less play a love song on it.

I had loved and lost Maria. However, as a result of The Law of Unintended Consequences, I had been introduced to what was to become one of the greatest loves of my life, playing the piano. Albert Camus once wrote something to the effect that people needed to love life; without the love of life, no meaning can console us. Playing piano was another way of loving life. In many respects, it was another way of dancing at the edge of Nietzsche's abyss. I was not sure exactly what dance Nietzsche was writing about, but I would choose something like a jig, probably one by Bach.

Playing piano is a joyful experience that may have no meaning beyond the moment. But it doesn't matter. Joy is sufficient unto that moment. So, thank you, Maria, wherever you are. I wish you love and happiness. I still think of you, admittedly less and less as the years have passed. But there still are those occasions when I try to catch a glimpse of you out of my peripheral vision while I'm seated at the keyboard. I look for you, and you are still young and lithe, your hair is golden, and your smile … sigh. But, as always, you continue to walk by me totally unaware that, over half a century ago, a boy loved you so much he learned to play the piano. And then I put my hands on the keyboard and begin playing "Maria."

Contrapunctus
by Marc Janssen

Exact			
Words			
Slip	*Words*		
Into	*Dark*		
Exact	*Lines*		
Place	*Join*		
Exact	*With*		
Words	*Symbols*	Sound	
Slip	*Words*	Over	
Into	*Dark*	Air	*While*
Exact	*Lines*	Sound	*New*
Place	*Join*	Words	*Meanings*
	With	Music	*Sing*
	Symbols	Sound	*While*
		Over	*New*
		Air	*Meanings*
		Sound	*Sing*
		Words	
		Music	

The Ditch

by Eileen Pettycrew

Time is a ditch of second-
hand treadmill and expired
aspirin, strand of chestnut
hair woven into robin's
nest, while a scalpel
excises a tumor, sand was
rock billions of years

ago and rock paper scissors
on the swim team bus raises red
welts on my arm as we rumble
past herky-jerky giant crickets
pumping oil from the ground
on a flat horizon where nothing
changes, ever; I will always
be on this bus. Yet blue-midnight

sky awakens, charcoal ghosts flee
at dawn, steam won't rise from cold
ocean but rises from sun-warmed soil
after spring rain—yes, before my eyes
steam rises, water cycles, tides tether
their yearning to the moon. Will I ever
be able to see the invisible? Meanwhile,
the ditch fills, spills

over, does not know
its limits, keeps packing in the perch
my father cleaned in the kitchen sink,
the red line forming behind the cut
of his knife, the white belly opened,
his hand scooping out purple
entrails, tap water washing
blood down the drain.

The Centerline
by Kaitlyn Burch

When my boyfriend, Silas, picked me up from work his brother, J.J., was with him. I worked at Alf's, that restaurant on 99W with the monkey. J.J. walked in first and Silas trailed behind, looking like he was real sorry, hands shoved in his pockets, blonde curls tucked behind his ears. My boss, Jerri, stood next to me at the cash register counting her money, and when the boys walked in she said, "Hot damn," and slapped my arm with a stack of ones.

The monkey, her name was Tonya, belonged to Jerri. She looked like the type of monkey people dressed in human clothes and put in movies and TV shows, small as your cat with wiry, brown hair. Jerri dressed her in special diapers made for preemie babies and jean shorts that hung to her knees. Customers liked to tap on the glass of Tonya's pen and marvel at how her hands looked like human hands and how funny her teeth were. No one ever said anything about how while they were eating their burgers, Tonya was probably sitting in her own mess.

J.J. walked right up to Tonya's cage and made monkey noises and tapped the glass.

Silas sat in one of the booths and put a quarter in the tabletop jukebox. I knew what he'd pick before the songs even came on: What a Wonderful World, My Way, and Stand By Your Man.

"You boys want a milkshake?" Jerri asked. "Make them a milkshake," she said to me.

Jerri had a big butt and short hair. She was always wearing t-shirts that read Willamette Valley or McMinnville, Oregon across her massive breasts, like she might forget where she was.

"I don't want a milkshake," Silas said from the booth, still looking through the songs.

Tonya's pen was a little room off to one side of the restaurant with a viewing window facing into the restaurant and another facing out to the patio. J.J. sat at the booth right next to Tonya's pen and watched her scamper around. "I'll take strawberry," he said.

"I just cleaned all the stuff," I said.

Jerri gave me a look as she walked back to her office. The first time she'd ever seen J.J. and Silas she said they look liked Greek gods, faces cut from marble. My mom said I should pray for J.J. because he wasn't handling the situation with his dad very well. I hadn't told my mom that I'd stopped praying.

J.J. and Silas' dad killed a man in a drunk driving accident back in January on Highway 22 between here and Salem. My mom had shown me the article about it in the News Register, as an example of the many perils of drinking. She'd found half a bottle of white wine hidden in my rolled-up sleeping bag. Missy Tangen had stolen it from her parents and she and I drank a cup each while our parents were at church bunko night. We mostly watched TV and asked each other intermittently: Do you feel anything? I tried to blame it all on Missy but my mom was convinced I was on the road to hell.

"Let her finish closing." Silas smiled at me.

"She can make a milkshake," J.J. said not looking over at us, eyes on Tonya. "Where's it sleep?"

"Jerri takes her home." I pulled the lid off the strawberry ice cream. "Let's her sleep in her bed," I said in a low voice, so Jerri couldn't hear.

"Such bullshit," J.J. said.

"What?" I asked.

"It shouldn't be on display."

"Jerri loves that monkey," Silas said, going to stand next to his brother. "It's like her kid."

"Would you put your kid in a cage?" J.J. asked.

"Where should she be?" I asked, running warm water over the ice cream scoop so it cut through the frozen pink, easy and smooth.

"The wild."

"Jerri got her off some farm in California."

"All the more reason," J.J. said.

Tonya placed her hand on the glass and J.J. leaned into the window, tapped at her little hand.

"Tonya wouldn't know how to live in the wild." I switched on the milkshake machine.

Over the whir of the wand I heard Silas laugh and say, "I forgot. Tonya. What a terrible name."

Jerri waved as we were leaving. She was stepping into Tonya's pen through the outside door. We climbed into Silas's truck and watched her walk across the parking lot with Tonya's arms wrapped around her neck.

"She carries it around like a baby," I said, sitting between Silas and J.J.

"It's sad," said Silas, starting the car.

"No, not sad." J.J. rolled his window down and lit a cigarette. "Sick." He nodded to the cage door as we drove away. "How's it lock?"

"I don't know. The handle?"

"We could steal that monkey," J.J. said, looking at his brother. He looked just like Silas, or Silas looked just like him. I couldn't tell. But J.J.'s curls were cut short and he was taller, or maybe that was just he way he carried himself, all pomp. "It'd be as easy as busting in on Silas taking a dump."

Silas reached across me to give J.J. a shove. "Shut up."

"Jerri would die of grief," I said, half kidding.

J.J. turned to look at me, eyes hot with hate or something like it. "Like you really care," he said.

Stopped at a light, J.J. threw his half-drunk milkshake out the window. It exploded across the asphalt, splashing on parked cars. At my house Silas walked me to the front door and kissed me. I dug my face into his armpit and smelled him, the musk that the musky deodorant couldn't cover up, spicy and ripe, made me want to push my hips into him. From the car, J.J. honked the horn.

I played soccer and worked at Alf's and got okay grades. My mom was a receptionist at a dentist's office and my dad worked as the church treasurer and part-time at the Community Center as the activities liaison, making sure the evening Jazzercise classes had an instructor.

Mr. Walker was the Walker of Walker Construction. I'd always spotted their trucks around town with the family name written across the door: WALKER CONSTRUCTION—WE BUILD IT RIGHT, and when I'd see Silas at school I'd think of those trucks, as if he were a gorgeous F-150 coming toward me.

My family attended Valley View Church of God, a non-denominational Christian church set up in the old Tri-Cinemas. They'd knocked out the walls and replaced the movie theater seats with wooden pews but left the screens. The concession counter was still there. I had suggested firing up the popcorn machine and selling bags for the services, proceeds going to charity, of course. My parents didn't see the humor in the idea. I knew then that I didn't believe in God, or Jesus, or Heaven, or Hell, but it was easier to keep going to church than to explain to my parents how none of it made sense to me anymore.

The Walkers had showed up at church two weeks after the accident. They rushed in late, just as Pastor Dan was welcoming everyone to the service and we were bowing our heads for the opening prayer. Mrs. Walker led her family down the aisle between pews, Silas behind her, then J.J. and last, Mr. Walker. I nudged my mom, who ignored me as if she were deep in prayer. The Walker's took the end of the row right in front of us. The boys spent the service looking uncomfortable and bored, sitting too long when asked to stand and standing too long when asked to sit. Mrs. Walker wore a bright pink dress and heavy gold bracelets that clung to her little wrists.

"Clothes too loud for church," my dad had commented.

Pastor Dan asked that we welcome them into our congregation and at coffee time, after the service, my mom went up and shook their hands, all of them, the boys too. My dad pretended that he needed to check something in the office and I stood awkward in my ugly church dress in the middle of the lobby on that movie theater carpet: film reels cascading down nothingness, a universe of red and green with purple stars.

Two weeks later Silas asked me on a date. I had been out before, but only with church boys whose desperation came out in sweaty palms and seemingly uncontrollable impulses to touch my breasts before even attempting to kiss me. My dad wanted me to have nothing to do with Silas, but my mom gave him a lecture about not punishing the son for the sins of the father and he relented, but offered this warning: Don't let that family ruin you.

In late May, the hills between Amity and McMinnville glow a deep green. With the windows rolled down, Silas and I drove out to his house. I had made it a practice to have Sunday dinner with the Walkers. Silas wanted me there. He'd told me I comforted him and I'd never been a comfort to anyone. Also, it upset my parents and I got some sort of pleasure thinking of them eating their meatloaf alone in silence. The Walker's house was large, on a property you couldn't see the edge of. I liked how far away it was from everything. Mr. Walker, still in his church clothes, walked to greet us, as we turned into the driveway. He had four months until his trial.

Mr. Walker loved his horses, and since Silas and I had been dating he'd tried to get me to ride.

"You want to ride today?" he asked me through Silas; he never spoke directly to me.

Silas rolled his eyes. "She doesn't want to ride, Dad."

Mr. Walker nodded, and looked at his son like he missed him before turning and walking toward the stables. Truthfully, I did want to ride, but Silas kept me pulled away from his dad. I didn't know what the Walkers were like before the accident, if they were all smiles and light, but after, it seemed like a large, strange quietness hung about them, as if they'd all retreated half a step back, covered in shadows.

In the house J.J. played *Call of Duty* in his dark bedroom. "How's that monkey?" he asked, eyes on the TV screen.

"You saw her last when I saw her last."

Silas grabbed a controller and I watched them play for forty-five minutes until Mrs. Walker called us to dinner. This was the fourth or fifth meal I'd had with them and no one made much attempt at small talk. Just to say something, Mrs. Walker told me she was considering going to the dentist my mom worked for because the one she saw made her gums bleed.

"You probably just need to floss more," I said.

J.J. laughed. "Jessie works at that burger place with the monkey," he said. "You can watch it while you eat and it wears this little diaper. I find monkey shit really appetizing. How about you guys?"

Mr. Walker ate his potatoes with a slow deliberation, staring at his son, as if eating the words.

Mrs. Walker reacted. "J.J.—not table talk."

Silas remained focused on his dinner. J.J. sat quiet for a moment and then asked if he could be excused and got up before anyone could answer.

Before the accident, I'd heard around school that Mr. Walker was tough. I never heard that he hit his kids, but that he was a serious man. The boys weren't athletes or particularly smart, but they enjoyed a type of status that money brings, throwing parties I was never invited to. From my very limited vantage point they both seemed to have it easy, and I thought my life might change when I started dating Silas, that I would be less ignored, that some of that ease might rub off on me. It was clear though; Silas had no ease to give.

The next Wednesday was slow at work. I sat alone at Alf's—except for

Tonya—taking quarters from the till, feeding the jukebox and staring at her monkey face. The freezers hummed and the grill's heat gave off a wet buzz, but no sound came through Tonya's pen.

She moved in graceful silence. I wondered what it'd like to be in there, sitting in her pen with her. I'd never touched her, held her, changed her diaper—Jerri did all that stuff. I wondered what it would be like to carry her around, hold her little body close to mine.

Tonya's walk had this rolling bounce to it and she never kept still for long. Even sitting, all wrapped up in the blanket Jerri'd gotten her from Wal-Mart, she fidgeted. She'd reach up into her jean shorts and scratch her butt then pull her fingers out and smell them, over and over. Then she'd stick one leg high in the air, long and straight and just hold it there like a ballerina. I found myself mimicking her movements, holding my head the way she held her head, moving my arms like she moved her arms.

Silas wandered in around eight. He pulled out a package of Drum that he said J.J.'d stolen from the 7-11 and suggested we go out back and roll cigarettes. Silas was better at keeping the tobacco uniform so I let him roll mine. I watched his mouth as he pulled little strings of tobacco from his tongue and lips. We stood in the parking lot, leaning against his truck, the door to Tonya's cage right in front of us.

"Would you get in trouble if one day she was just gone?" he said.

I looked at him, that deep V of his t-shirt, his unzipped hoodie, his Adam's apple moving up and down. "I don't know. I guess it would depend on whether or not I stole her."

Silas stepped toward the door, cigarette dangling from his lip. "Is it locked now?"

I laughed to cover an urge to jump out and stop him. "I don't know."

He grabbed the handle and shook it.

"Don't open it," I said.

"Why?"

"What if she ran out?"

He put his cigarette out on his shoe, threw the butt into the bushes. "J.J. wants that monkey."

"I thought he wanted to set her free."

"He wants her for something." He grabbed my hands and pulled me to him. "Something to do. I guess."

"I'd get in trouble," I said into his chest. "Jerri would freak out."

"I don't want you to get in trouble."

I believed him. Somewhere down the street a door slammed, a child shrieked with delight. The parking lot smelled like grease and char-burgers. It was after eight and still light out and somewhere, just a few weeks away, summer was coming.

On Saturday I was supposed to go into work at three but I got a call from Jerri at ten asking me to come down to Alf's. I'd known the call was coming, had been up half the night waiting for the phone to ring. My mom dropped me off and saw two cops looking into Tonya's cage.

"Looks like trouble," she said giving me a meaningful look.

Jerri greeted me with a hug, pressing her large breasts into my body.

The night before, Jerri had called to say that she wasn't coming in, that she was staying over at the coast, and that Tonya would be fine for the night in her pen. I was working with LaShea, this too thin girl from Yamhill who wore too much make-up and wild earrings. We just needed to make sure the door was locked, and the A/C was off—to keep it jungle-like. When Jerri told me this I'd been leaning against the wall by the corkboard where notices for summer festivals were posted, rules about minimum wage, and washing your hands covered by stupid monkey comic strips. The plastic of the phone was sticky at my ear, the heat from the grill made everything sweat. When Jerri told me this I felt like the universe was putting its arm around me, squeezing me to it, and telling me I was capable of things, and later Silas walked in and looked so beautiful and I saw LaShea look him up and down from under her heavily painted eyelids. Jerri had asked me twice if I understood and I'd said, "Of course."

So when I was off that night I sat in Silas' truck and said, "Jerri isn't coming for Tonya tonight." And he just looked at me. "She's at the coast or something." I swallowed hard, wanting to be fully aware of the choice I was making. "The door's unlocked," I said.

So when Jerri was squatting next to me holding my hand like she was going to propose or something, and said, "I'm not mad, but did you check to see if the cage was locked before you left?" I had rehearsed my answer, stayed up late practicing in the mirror so I was ready to lie and say, "I'm sure I did."

Jerri looked at me, relieved, and hugged me again. "Of course you did," she said.

Kaitlyn Burch

I told the cops the same thing: I locked the door. I got a ride home with my boyfriend.

I even told them that Silas and I drank wine and smoked cigarettes in the driveway of my parent's house to make it seems like I was scared and would tell them anything. They asked a lot of questions: Did I notice anything peculiar as I was leaving? Had there been anyone snooping around the last few days, watching the monkey? I suggested that maybe Tonya herself opened the door to her cage, because weren't monkeys supposed to be smart like that?

All night, customers asked after Tonya. Why was her cage empty? Where was she? And we told them that she was home with Jerri. We had to force Jerri to leave. It was like she was waiting for Tonya to come walking back in her little diaper and jean shorts. A lady from the News Register came and I told her she should talk to Jerri, not me. But LaShae couldn't wait to be quoted. She sat the lady down and told her everything she knew, which took all of thirty seconds. Then she gave the lady a chocolate malt on the house.

I snuck glances at Tonya's empty cage. It was painted to resemble what an elementary schooler might think a jungle looked like. Green grass and trees lined the walls and animals lurked in the brush: tiger, lion, some zebra stripes. It was so lame. Toys for Tonya to climb hung from the ceiling and the gross tile floor, that generic school cafeteria kind, was littered with her monkey biscuits, these dried up crackers Tonya gnawed on all day. I didn't think that cage could get any more depressing, but looking at it that night, empty and dark, I realized that things could always get worse.

After we'd closed and were wiping the tables with bleach solution, LaShae said, "I wonder what Tonya's doing right now." She looked up, searching the furthest reaches of her brain.

Part of me wished that Tonya had given one big monkey jump, clasped the metal doorknob and pulled it down with all her weight to waddle out and meet the warm spring night. But I knew J.J. had her. I knew Silas was with him. And I knew I hadn't locked the door.

After work, Silas and I headed out of town toward his house. He said, "It wouldn't have mattered. J.J. would have broken in."

"I feel like I should feel worse than I do," I said and hated myself a little. "He says he wants to sell her."

"Sell her?" The words swelled in my throat, made my tongue heavy. The wave of regret I'd been waiting for hit hard and all I could do was sit in it. "I thought he was going to set her free. Or keep her as a pet."

"He won't actually do it."

"What will he do?"

Silas was driving too fast. He didn't turn on his brights and I could only see fifteen feet in front of us. "I don't know," he said.

I watched the light on the road. As each foot of pavement became illuminated I expected something to jump in front of us—a raccoon, a deer, a man. "Can I have a cigarette?" I asked.

He handed me the pack of tobacco. "You'll have to roll it."

"Forget it," I said, tossing it on the dash.

Silas' hands choked the wheel. "We'll convince him to take her back," he said. "Say it was a joke."

I leaned my head against the window. "We can't take her back," I said and stared into the blackness. The window was cold on my forehead. I knew there were fields and orchards spreading from the road, all the way to where the black of the earth met the black of the sky. "Do you guys need money or something?" I asked and turned to look at his profile, the strong nose, the cheekbones.

"People don't want murderers building houses for them," he said like he was reporting it, had heard it from someone else—his dad, or J.J.

We were way out of town now, in the in between, the farmland. "He's not a murderer," I said. Mr. Walker had crossed the centerline, pulled into those few inches of space that separated us in this waking world from those in the other.

"You know what he said?" Silas asked me. "When he was sitting in the police car waiting to go to jail that day after the accident?"

"What?"

"He said, 'I know he's dead. I know I killed him. Please kill me.'"

"How do you know he said that?"

"He told us. He admitted to everything. He told us he wants to be clean and forgiven.

Why do you think we showed up at your church?"

"It's a good thing, right? Forgiveness?" I said, falling back on my Christian upbringing.

"If you think that's the way it works," Silas said.

Tonya was in a small dog cage in the barn. The door of the cage hung open; her little human hands wrapped around the bars. J.J. sat next to the cage, watching her, feeding her apple slices. His eyes were bright and wild, the most alive I'd ever seen them look. "I just opened the door and she came to me," he said. "She wrapped her arms around my neck and held on." He looked at me completely different than he had before, like I'd passed some test. We were friends now. "Want to hold her?" he asked.

A bare bulb hung over us, strung up by an extension cord. It lit the barn in a harsh yellow. Bales of hay stood stacked against the walls, and where the light stopped, where the perfect pool ended—there was darkness. The barn smelled like hay and dirt and wood. I did want to hold Tonya, but before I could even answer J.J. was offering her to me, passing her over like an infant. I put my arms under her, cradling her, and she nestled her body against me. Her hair was coarse and thick on her back and thinner on her face. I looked down into her little animal eyes.

"She's really smart," J.J. said. "She figured out how to open the door of the dog cage."

Silas reached over and scratched her back. "She just likes hanging out. She's like a little dude."

I pulled her off me, taking her hands in mine and held her away from me, off the ground, like a sheet I was about to fold. Her hands felt human wrapped around my fingers. She held on tight, looking up at her long arms, sticking out her tongue. J.J. had taken off her jean shorts and her diaper. It was the first time I had seen her bare, as nature intended. She started to swing back and forth and I played along, moving my arms with her motion. She was putting on a show for us and with an ache I felt rotten, thinking about Jerri, about her sitting at home watching TV with some old afghan draped over her lap, missing this.

"You won't sell her?" I asked.

J.J. looked over at Silas. "Maybe," he said.

"Why?" I stopped swinging Tonya, let her feet hit the ground. She kept a hold of one of my hands and I walked her around the barn, the hay soft under my feet. She waddled.

"Why not?" said J.J.

I was frustrated and near tears, "Because you said," was my weak offering.

J.J. looked blank and then the barn door slid open. Tonya and I both turned to see Mr. Walker standing in the warm, dark night. He was dressed like he was going to work: Carhartt pants, button-down flannel, and boots, even though it was well passed eleven. I don't know what compelled him to come out to the barn but he looked from Tonya to me a few times, his hands in his back pockets, weight on one hip. He didn't appear surprised or mad. His eyes finally rested on J.J., then Silas.

"Where'd you get that monkey?" he said. He didn't look at me, but kept him eyes on his sons.

J.J. wouldn't look up, but Silas looked at me, embarrassed. Neither boy said anything, neither looked at their dad. I felt it then, all lit up in that barn—the cold emptiness of disappointment, of wanting so much to take something back. Mr. Walker just kept looking at his sons, like he knew them, like he could look at them forever. Tonya screeched a little, tugged on my arm and walked toward Mr. Walker.

"You probably aught to be gettin' home," he said, speaking directly to me for the first time. "And make sure that monkey gets home too." Then he turned and walked back toward the house.

Jerri didn't press charges. She knew about Mr. Walker and the trouble he was in and she knew that Silas and J.J. were messed up because of it. She fired me though, and LaShae, and I let her fire LaShae even though LaShae didn't do anything wrong. Fury didn't aptly describe my parent's rage. My dad insisted that I break up with Silas, and I told him that I did—but I didn't, not right away anyway. I was still holding out for something, some quiver of danger or difference.

I was unemployed for a few weeks before I got a job at Video Yogurt Express and told my parents the owner needed me to open Sunday mornings so I didn't have to go to church anymore. I spent Sunday mornings watching Breakfast at Tiffany's and eating baby cones of chocolate yogurt. Sometimes, I missed Tonya.

Silas and I finally broke up in late July, on the porch of my parents' house, on one of the hottest days of the year. It was me who did the breaking. After we returned Tonya, I guess the boys and their dad had some huge talk and J.J. got past his "acting out phase" and he and Silas both got really serious about God and forgiveness, probably thinking about how their dad was going to go to prison. J.J. planned to go on a mission in the fall instead of college and I started to feel like the only things I'd liked about Silas were the way his jeans hung from his hips and the strength of his hands. Silas was a good guy, too good for me I realized, and I was sure he'd become one of those gorgeous camp counselors at Wi-Ne-Ma that all the girls dropped their panties for.

A few weeks before his trial, on a warm September night, Mr. Walker committed suicide. I heard Silas found him strung up in their barn by an extension cord. I felt like I knew this was going to happen, like I'd conjured it in some way, and when I heard about it I was somehow relieved, like I had felt his guilt and then I was free of it. I could see him hanging, could picture him climbing those bales of hay, tying the cord around the timber beam, and then his neck.

My mom cut the obituary from the paper and we attended the funeral together. My dad refused to go, said he wouldn't mourn the loss of a coward. My mom told him that wasn't very Christian of him and I was proud of her for saying so.

At the funeral there was a slide show of pictures: Mr. Walker as a young man, smiling on a beach; Mr. Walker holding baby Silas, or maybe baby J.J. Toward the end, after the pictures and more praying, the people who'd known Mr. Walker far better than I had, and better than most members of the church had, the people who knew him as a regular guy, not someone who'd killed a man with his car, those people stood up and told stories about what great guy he was. Then a girl sang "Amazing Grace" and I grabbed my mom's hand. She said something about him being at peace. I thought she was right. Wherever he was, he didn't feel bad about what he'd done anymore. Like I said, I didn't believe in Heaven or Hell or God or Jesus, but something about that song—the part about saving a wretch like me—tore me up.

Editor's Note: Alf's Restaurant and its monkey are real, but everything else in the story is a work of fiction.

Whispers
by Marilyn Johnston

My husband has hearing loss
in his right ear. He says
it's another part of him
that went missing
after Vietnam—
the result of a concussion
from a discharging Howitzer
just before the end
of his tour.

I've never felt the shock wave
from a Howitzer's blast—
only the crack from
an old front-loaded musket
my high school riflery coach
allowed us to shoot
along the Appomattox,
deep in the woods.
I recall each time the barrel
recoiled, the butt of the gun
as it jolted my shoulder,
leaving its mark;
the shot as it reverberated
off the hills around me.

When his nightmares come,
I whisper in my husband's
wounded ear, hoping he can
make out my words—
as if the familiar sound
would penetrate
through enemy lines
and reach him,
pulling him across.

Olly Olly Oxen Free
by Laura LeHew

1.
I google you and find you dead or a health hazard
or a former athlete or linked-in or face-booked (but I'm not)
also possibly wearing tight tan slacks
(which only you could pull off)

I google you and find out that you never
won a Senior National title in Olympic lifting
that there are similar people in places like Humble,
Kouts, Cheshire and Groom

I find pictures, your dead wife
but I never find you

2.
I grapevine you
get your 411
listen as your peeps
shout out
911

3.
you grab my hand
pull me near
whisper

I'm your knight
your white horse
I will always be there

4.
olly olly

Passage Money
by John Byrne

66Keep looking until you find her." Grandma yelled into the phone. I
knew she was yelling at Dad. It was the same thing she had yelled at him
when he got home and she wouldn't let him in the house. He had to go
right back out even though he didn't want to and it was rainy and cold.

"She wants to be found." Grandma screeched. "Haven't I lived with my
daughter thrice as long as you? Her in her fancy blue dress and all despite
the devil's own wind and rain. She wants to be found, I'm telling you."

Marie and I lay on our tummies in front of the living room fire like
we always did on Fridays but we didn't feel like saying anything and there
was no one in the three chairs that made a half ring around the fireplace.
Grandma had been in her chair after she chased Daddy back out into the
rain and she had stayed there and said she had to watch us even though I
was a boy and almost nine and knew what to do around fires. Grandma had
sat there and rocked in that rocker with the carved wooden dragons on each
side until the kitchen phone rang and she pushed herself up. "Stay there."
she ordered as she left us alone for the first time.

We heard her voice through the wall and we heard the wind clattering
the windows and sometimes the wind came down the chimney, pushing
the flames out toward us. We only had the big old radio to play with and
we had to move the dial because all the stations dodged around whenever
there was a storm in Montauk, even during the World Series, since the wind
pushed them around. I was the one who usually did the dial but Marie did
sometimes, too, as the voice we kept on losing and looking for talked loudly
about that big boat, the Andrea boat, that was in real trouble in the same
storm off Montauk that was making the station dodge around all the time.

"There she is." The radio voice was very excited. "Oh my God, she's cut
almost in half." I twisted the dial to catch up with the disappearing voice
and I shot right over it and I had to twist slowly back and it said, "It is sink-
ing, for sure. Oh, my God, it is sinking." Then the voice was lost.

Marie said, "Find it," but I was already trying and we could still hear
Grandma shouting into the phone, saying, again and again, "She wants to

be found. That's why she does these things."

We knew the Andrea was a big ocean liner because the radio had said that and the radio had said it was full of important people because it had just left New York City and now it was sinking.

"It is sinking." I whispered, talking to Marie for the first time since the door slammed. "It is sinking the way that Lucy boat that Grandma told us about sank when she was a child in Ireland and did not have any shoes."

Marie was quiet and then she said that if the Andrea boat was like the Lucy boat, then there would be dresses, lots of dresses floating and floating on the ocean waves the way Grandma had said there had been when that other boat sank. "And," Marie said, "there would be passage money, the way there had been and we could find it and take it and go someplace wonderful."

I stared at Marie and it was not impolite because she stared at me and then we both got up off our tummies and tiptoed to the side door, pushing it open and not stopping even when the wind smacked us right in the face, ripping away every bit of the fireplace heat. I took Marie's hand in case she was scared and we crept across the porch. We leaped down onto the sand path that we had followed a million times through the up-and-down dunes and the scratchy-dune grass to the crumbly edge where the ocean waves reached toward you.

We pressed close to each other but my eyes teared up from the wind as we waited for things to appear from the dark the way they do if you waited long enough.

I wanted to see the dresses. I expected to see Mommy's blue dress, too, and I could see in my mind the lift and flow that the skirt part made when she danced, like a tent big enough to crawl inside. I didn't say anything like that to Marie because Marie had cried when the door slammed and I thought that saying something might make her cry again. Marie had stopped crying when Grandma picked the note off the floor and told her to stop crying even though Grandma wouldn't read the note. Instead, Grandma got mad.

That happened before Daddy came from the Friday afternoon train and was chased out of the house by Grandma. "You go right out now and find her."

Daddy left so fast he did not even remember to give us the Friday newspaper he brought from the City so I could read Marie the comics.

Mommy had to be going to an important place, an adult important place, otherwise she would not have had to leave and when the radio said that the Andrea boat was a boat full of important people, I thought maybe that was where she had been going even if Grandma did not know it. I did not know why Grandma was so mad about it because she went to important adult places too, sometimes, and told us about some of them.

Marie and I peered and peered from the dune's edge but the wind was full of rain and mist off the crests of the huge waves and we did not see anything. No Andrea boat, no dresses, nothing but the heave of black waves and the coiled white foam that sprang from them. Marie shone the flashlight she had swiped from beside the porch door but its light shattered in the damp darkness and Grandma was suddenly right there beside us.

"Isn't it enough that your crazy mother has run away again?" she hollered. "Do you two have to torment me as well?" She dragged us toward the empty house where the porch door hung open, spilling room light into the wind.

I saw a light appear and disappear in the spray and I said it must be the boat and Grandma said, "Don't be stupid. That's the lighthouse. You cannot see any boats from here."

I did not say that I thought I heard screams in the wind and I could almost make out the words and I thought maybe I heard my mother's voice among them and that made me very scared. And I didn't say anything about the dresses or the passage money even though it was Grandma who had told us in the first place.

Grandma had told us many times. She always began by saying that she had been a shoeless child who, unlike the two of us, did not get to eat all the time. And she always said that despite it all, when she was walking the dirt paths of Dunquin and Ballyferriter, she appreciated everything she had which I did not understand because she also said she had had nothing.

Grandma told us of waking to the sun rising over Mount Eagle and hearing the neighbors say that there were riches covering the sea from Slea Head all the way to Inishnabro even before the radio at the store told about the Boat Lucy and the nasty Germans and the terror felt by the rich people sinking into the cold, black ocean. Grandma ran to the shore, where she perched on the sharp black rocks that go far out into the waves and could smash an unwary boat and she saw an eternity of dresses floating peacefully in the morning light and she began pulling them in.

John Byrne

Grandma did not tell us anything as she dragged us back across the dunes. She shoved us toward the fireplace, saying, "Stay there this time." We lay down on our tummies still shaking from the rain and the cold until the flames chased them off. Daddy was not there in his chair because he was still on the other end of the phone, listening as Grandma said, "Yes, they are all right." And then she said, "Sometimes I swear they are more like their mother than they ought to be."

Next, there was silence, which meant that Grandma was listening and then Grandma raised her voice, "She wants to be found. That's why she does these things."

Daddy must have disagreed because Grandma got really mad. "Don't you think I know her after all the trouble she has been?" Grandma did not tell Daddy that he had forgotten to leave the newspaper for us.

We lay on our tummies and I reached for the radio and twisted the dial and heard the voice. "There are people falling into the sea." Then the voice dodged away leaving only static and the wind battering the windows and banging tree branches against the house.

Grandma sat in her rocker in the half-circle around the fire and she said, "I don't know why you children are trying to listen to that thing." But she did not tell us to turn it off. Grandma said, "Your mother will drive me crazy." I wanted to say that was not true but I was afraid. Instead, I moved the dial carefully some more and caught up to the voice but it did not say anything more about people falling into the sea, only about lights and how they were going out one at a time. The voice never did say anything about dresses.

Grandma's brother, Padraig, who is our great uncle and whose name means Patrick and who sometimes acts really strange, told Marie and me one time that there had been bodies in the sea from the Lucy, just the way the radio voice said you could see bodies in the waves off Montauk, only Padraig said that the bodies were bloated soft, white bodies of the rich people and everyone on the shore had to pull and tug to get the clothes off but Grandma said, "Hush up. You are going to disturb the children."

And then Grandma said there were no bodies, just dresses flowing on the quiet green-blue water and there were some life rings and pieces of wood but there were no bodies. Padraig made a snorting noise and Grandma said, again, "Hush up." I thought as I lay before the fire that maybe Uncle Padraig had been at the ocean at night when there had been bodies but in the morning when Grandma was on the shore, there were only dresses on the gentle waves.

That was when I understood. Marie and I had been wrong to go out into the night because it was in the morning that the dresses would appear as they had appeared in the ocean off Kerry all the way from Slea Head to Inishnabro.

I elbowed Marie when Grandma went back again to the ringing phone and before Marie could shriek, "Ow!" I said, of course we could not see the dresses because it was still night and the Andrea was still going down and we had to wait until the sun rose.

The radio voice then reported that there were still lights in the water and Grandma shouted into the phone, "It's no good for her unless she gets found ... All that stuff in the note about having her own life was just childish crap ... Don't I know her better than you?"

"How much money will be in the dresses," Marie asked and I said I did not know. I only knew that Grandma had said there had been passage money in the Lucy's dresses. Marie asked what passage money was because she said she forgot and I told her it was how the Irish paid to go from Kerry to Boston to get away from the British who had stolen all the land and forced the Irish to eat seaweed but Marie said she knew all about that and that she only wanted to know now how much there would be and I said again that I didn't know but that it had to be a lot because Grandma paid for passage and there was money left over for her to buy and sell land in Boston and that had made her so rich that she always sailed the way the rich people did on the Lucy, first class, with servants around all the time to give her everything she wanted.

"Where was the money in the dresses," Marie asked, "because dresses don't have pockets."

I said that I don't know but maybe they had pockets back then.

I had once asked Uncle Padraig where the passage money was in the dresses and he had laughed and laughed and said pirates could find money in anything and I thought that he meant the money was hidden in the cloth someplace like in a seam or something the way that Grandma said she hid money when she was younger. I did not know who the pirates were and when I asked Grandma who Uncle Padraig was talking about she got really mad and said Padraig was a bitter old man and there were no pirates in Kerry, only decent folk starved by the British. Padraig heard her and whispered that some of those decent folk would hang out phony lights to lure boats onto the sharp black rocks and even though Padraig had whispered, Grandma heard and said he was drunk and that he should leave the wee ones alone. I knew that we were the wee ones but I never learned the truth about the pirates.

Marie asked me again how we would figure out where the passage money was and I could only answer that it would be obvious and she was satisfied. I hoped I was right because I did not want to ask Grandma even though she was back in her rocker above us because she had finished yelling at Dad. Instead, I thought of Mommy's blue dress, thinking that the money could not be along the bottom of the skirt or the skirt would not have floated out like a big tent that I could get into when she twirled.

Grandma was silent as she rocked above us and I wanted to say something but before I could think of what to say, the phone rang again and Grandma got up. "Don't move an inch, you two," she said.

We could hear Grandma through the wall. "Well then check the Negro bars, too.

That would be just like her, going where she does not belong."

I wanted to ask why Daddy did not go out to the Andrea boat just as the radio voice shrieked that the bow was breaking off and it was going down and there were life boats rocking all around on the swells and people bobbing around with lights in the water and that was when I got truly afraid because I thought Mommy might be lost. I said to myself that it would be all right because in the morning everything would be all right, because mornings were always quiet after storms and everyone was polite.

"Don't come back," Grandma roared into the phone, "until you find her."

Grandma came back to the fire and asked if she had to do everything but she didn't seem to expect any answer.

I still thought I should say something so I asked Grandma to tell the story of the Normandy boat that she had taken when it zigzagged all the way from London to New York to escape the Germans, who were starting another war. She was proud of being on that boat but this time Grandma said that things were so different now and not better at all.

I said that maybe the Andrea boat should have zigzagged from New York to avoid being hit by that boat with the ordinary name but Grandma said I was mixing things up again and that I didn't understand. Then the phone rang.

"Well, where are you?" Grandma asked again and again. "No, I won't be your messenger and I won't put them on the phone. You get back here where you belong this very instant."

Something happened and Grandma put the phone slowly down just as we caught up with the radio voice again and it said that the stern part was now going down and the lifeboats were trying to pull away so as not to be caught in the drag and I knew that Mommy wouldn't be sucked down because she had made that phone call.

Marie twisted the dial as the voice slipped away and then she stopped and asked me why the passage money didn't sink the dresses and I said it was obvious and she would understand in the morning but it worried me because I did not know how we would find the dresses if they sank to the bottom because I could not hold my breath for long when I swam. I repeated that it would be obvious.

Grandma came back as I said the word "obvious" and she asked what was obvious and I was afraid she would get mad if I told her what I had said so I only said that it was obvious that the Andrea boat was going down as Marie found the radio voice again and the radio voice said it was all over, the stern had slid beneath the water, making a huge wave that was overturning many of the lifeboats and more and more people were in the sea. We were all silent and Marie started crying and I said that there was nothing to worry about, that it would be all right and Grandma said I was an idiot just like my mother and I did not argue with her because I was happy. I knew Mommy would be all right. Marie got quiet as I held her and she fell asleep in front of the fire.

The wind rattled all the windows and began banging that loose drain pipe that Daddy had promised to fix and I asked Grandma if they would survive, meaning the people in the lifeboats, but she must have thought I was talking about Mommy and she said, "She'll be back. She is angry, sure, but she will be back."

I did not know what else to say so we were silent except for the fire, the wind, and the radio voice, which now said a new boat was plucking people from the sea like fish meaning that the people were like fish and I wondered if Mommy would smell of seaweed but I was probably asleep when I wondered that for I always wonder strange things just as I fall asleep.

I woke in my bed the next morning. I tiptoed to Marie's room. She was waiting for me and we crawled out her window and across the porch roof, past Mommy and Daddy's room where there was only one lump in the bed and it was too small to be two people and we went down the tree on the side of the porch and then across the dunes on the same path to the ocean beyond. The ocean was very calm.

We stood on the top of the dunes and we shaded our eyes against the rising sun and we squinted and squinted and there was nothing for us to see.

The Turning
by Eileen Pettycrew

1.

Drugged with dusk's perfume.
She stands on the picnic table
while aunts pack up Kool-Aid,
fried chicken, potato salad, ice box cookies.
The wheel turns in violet light
and back, back she walks.

2.

Hard scrappy grass catches her flat.
Above her, faces float in a circle,
as her left upper arm screams
hidden white-hot skeleton.

3.

She tells no one.
A priest of fire in a mandolin dress
coaxed her backward on a lean branch of heaven,
her phantom basket of fish leaning
orange in the disappearing light,
corpse of her death mirrored
in the painter's atlas, handful of shadow
thrown on the canvas:
crack in the bone opening her eyes
opening
her eyes.

Hero
by Cristina White

I. The Fine Dust of the Road

This is what I remember: A young man standing quietly to one side of my brother's workbench, watching him match the corners of beveled wood for a picture frame. The young man isn't tall, but his body is solid, rooted; he has a presence. Skin darkened by the sun, brown hair and deep brown eyes, arms and chest swelled with hard muscle, and a face that is plainly beautiful.

This is what I remember of being seventeen: coming home from school, and there he is, in a black tee shirt and jeans, suddenly in my life.

"This is Art," my brother, Henry says. "He's going to stay with us a while, and help out."

Art says softly, "Hello."

He's shy, I think, like me.

I don't ask him anything. Where he is from, how he knows Henry. He looks tired, worn from his travels. I imagine brushing the hair from his forehead, seeing the fine dust of the road drift in the sunlit air around him, drift and come to rest on his strong shoulders.

Whenever I can, I keep Art company. I love his steady, quiet way, such a contrast to Henry's flamboyant confident, wit, and sudden bursts of laughter. I try to win Art's friendship. I share my hopes and aspirations, and I ask him about his dreams, what he sees in his future, but he seldom speaks about himself. Instead, he listens. I notice that about him, the way he listens to people. He absorbs whatever we share with him; he breathes in our stories and carries them deep inside his veins. It may be that our stories are like places, a part of his travels.

It seems to me that he doesn't believe that he will stay here, in Henry's ample house. Art belongs to the road, and one day he'll be gone.

It doesn't matter. I love him.

II. *The Edge of the Garden*

This is what I remember: A warm summer evening, and a party spilling out from the house into a mild June night. Laughter and music, voices and conversation. I thread my way through the people and go outside. I walk across the grass until the voices dim behind me, and I find Art alone, sitting on the stone steps at the edge of the garden.

I sit with him and we begin to talk. I know that tonight, this fragrant, starlit night, I have to say what I feel. I have to confess that I love him. And so I do. I tell him. And he is kindest then, in that moment. He speaks slowly, searching for words, struggling with the truth until; finally, he has only his honesty to give me. He cares for me, he says, and cares about me, but the truth is that he loves my brother. His heart belongs to Henry, who is nine years older than me. Henry is my half brother, my mother's only son. Long before I was born, he became part of another family, and we have grown up separately. These last two years in Berkeley mark the first time we have lived in the same house. I am still learning who Henry is.

Art is beside me on the stone steps, the revelation of his love still lingering in the summer air. Now I understand why he seems so sad this evening, sitting apart, by himself, while Henry holds court inside the house. I see in a new light the charm of the young men who are a part of my brother's life. At last, I comprehend that Art and Henry are more than friends. They are lovers.

III. *The Gift of Understanding*

This is what I remember: After opening my heart to him, after hearing what he feels for my brother, Art and I are truly friends. He no longer has to ask himself how to guide my love and desire toward someone else, and I can love him without wondering how to win a way into his arms. That is not to be.

Art has given me something I needed far more than romance. He has given me the truth, and with that, the gift of understanding. Now Henry's scattered outbreaks of intense emotion make sense, and all the relationships fall into place. Though I don't talk to Henry about my newfound knowledge, I feel at peace with him as never before, and free.

This is what I remember: We are at another party, at the home of one of Henry's best friends, who is a slender man with hair graying at the temples.

The man lives with his mother in a big, beautiful house not far from us. The entire ground floor of the house is an antique shop. Out in front is a small parking lot for customers. Tonight, the lot is filled with the cars of their friends. It's a mild autumn evening. There's music, laughter, food, drink. People talking, telling jokes.

My stepfather, Blair, is at the party too; he is recently returned from a tour of duty in Korea. The whole year that he was gone, I had luxuriated in the time with my mother, free of anxiety. I had not had to steel myself against the explosive arguments between my parents. Their terrible fights.

But Blair is back now, and we are at the party. I'm standing with a small group of people, listening to the voices around me, when something catches my attention—something I hear, or sense, that causes me to turn and scan the room. I realize that my mother is nowhere in sight. She is gone. Blair is gone. And, suddenly, I remember being eleven years old, in a tavern on a winter night long ago, a tavern room like this room, noisy with people who are drinking and talking. Then, like now, I looked up to see that my mother was gone. Blair was gone.

As I did then, I make my way through the crowd. I step outside to a veranda that looks out over the parking lot. When I was eleven, I gazed out at a parking lot from the doorway of the tavern. It was snowing. Tonight, there is a sliver of a moon in a clear sky. The season has changed. The nightmare is the same.

There, in the shadows and streetlight, I see Blair and my mother. Blair is two hundred pounds, six feet tall, and drunk. He's cursing my mother, pounding her with his voice. He is only seconds away from pounding her with his fists, that moment when he will beat a woman who barely comes up to his chest.

It's happening again, the nightmare repeated throughout the years, the thing he has said he will never do again, as he professes his love and begs forgiveness. Never again, he swears. Never. He strikes, breaking skin and trust and a promise. But this time his fist only finds its mark once. My mother cries out and from the darkness Art emerges, not very tall, but solid, rooted, muscled, his quiet demeanor turned now into a cold fury. He pushes my stepfather back, away from my mother, and challenges him to hit some-one who can hit back. But Art doesn't wait for Blair's stunned response. He throws a clean, hard punch and hits Blair with the full force of a rage that comes from deep inside him. He hits Blair hard, and Blair goes down, arms and legs jerking; he falls to the ground. I watch Art put his arm around my mother's shoulders, speak to her gently, and lead her away from her husband, sprawled on the cement.

The child in me, who has longed so many times to rescue my mother, who prayed and prayed for this marriage to be over, the fifteen year old girl filled with hatred for her stepfather, wrapping her hand around a big kitchen knife and contemplating murder—all those moments, all those years, all that futility and sorrow and desperation—are now released. In one act, in one brave, true act, Art has stepped up for my mother, for me, and settled the score.

V. Innocent Girls and Tender Young Men

This I can't remember: What became of Art. That memory is indistinct. I only know it didn't work out between Henry and him, and one day it was time for him to go, back to the road that owned him. In the tangle of lives, the intersection of lovers, husbands and wives, innocent girls and tender young men, the complexity of love overlaid and undercut by bitterness and shadow, Art will remain in memory, bearing my gratitude and love, and defined by two events, two choices that he made: One summer evening when he told the truth, and set me free, one autumn night, when he protected my mother, and again, set me free.

I remember him always, pure kindness, pure rage, pure hero.

My Happy Family: Two Versions
by Donna Henderson

1.

With our father, we would head for the hills for good. We'd pack in sides of
bacon and bags of beans. The guard station at Bagby would be our home;
we would make it our business to guard the woods. We would make do with
what we had, wearing pioneer clothing; we would use ingenuity to make
the forest our home. We would cook on the iron stove, haul water from the
spring. We would forage for wood sorrel, wild onions and fiddleheads; we'd
learn other wild foods and would use these too. I would play the guitar and
we would sing in the evening: Woody Guthrie, Irish ballads, Wild Mountain
Thyme. We would bathe in a tub we'd hacked out of a cedar log, hotsprings
water sluicing through a hollowed-out limb. Our mother wouldn't be there
but that was not the dream's problem; we'd love our life every day and we
would all get along. Hikers would come sometimes, just passing through;
they would say hello, wish they were us and go. The first winter storm
would come when we were sleeping. We would wake to high snow, low sky,
the dawn's thin light between them. We would wake to the silence of buried
trails.

2.

We would purchase, to live in, my elementary school building. We would
move in and kick out the kids and staff. We would choose our own rooms
and I'd make mine in the library, wedging my bed in between the stacks.
We would twirl in the empty halls, screech and yell when we wanted; our
mother wouldn't be bothered in her distant room. We'd take over the music
room and learn all of the instruments; mom would play the piano and we'd
all sing along. We'd take over the kitchen and drum on the steel counters,
We would marvel and revel in the vast supplies. There'd be creamed corn,
Spagetti-Os, green beans and Bac-O-Bits; we'd eat cherry pie filling out of
#10 tins. We'd be inventive with Velveeta, fishsticks, ketchup and Bisquick;
there'd be more food than we'd need for the rest of our lives. We'd use the
cafeteria's tables for our arts and crafts projects; we would skate on its tile

in our stockinged feet. Outside, we would so own playground and swingset, without mean kids to tease us when our underpants showed. Our father didn't appear but that was not the dream's business, our mother so happy with us, alone.

A Taste of Place
by K. F. Hanson

The soil is barren here,
so unforgiving that in long ago times, not even marsh grasses grew.
The ground takes the water deep into itself here,
so that the roots of all living things must go the full distance to drink it,
to pull it up, up, up all the long way into themselves unassisted
and then in a single rush, to take it, take it all the way in.
There's no comfort here,
no evening out in what's below.
The ground has salt from the sea here
and the salt lies deep in the clay.

We stand oldest to youngest
arranged in a row,
and wait for justice.
Justice is what he calls it,
evening out the score,
coming to Jesus,
turning water into wine.

Teach you girls a lesson
Teach you girls a thing or two
Teach you all about uppity
and not what you think you are

He pats the rope, the belt, the snake-headed switch
against one palm and looks down the line,
oldest to youngest,
first seed to last,
no blinking, no weeping, no noise.

There's a vineyard not far from here,

where the finest of wine grapes grow.
The best of the wines, they say,
comes from clay and cold nights and salt.
Where the water must be pulled from deep down unassisted,
to bathe in the yeast of the skin,
'til the vines grow thin with the effort
and flesh finds a power within.

Teach you girls a lesson
Teach you girls a thing or two
Oldest to youngest, arranged in a row,
we are body into blood, and blood into wine,
oh, the alchemy of wine.

The Killing Jar
by Michael Newman

Rosie leaps into the spring air, her back arched, a butterfly net held above her like a samurai sword. Downward she swings and engulfs the elusive butterfly. As she hits the ground, she holds the net out in front so not to crush her prize. She has captured a rare Karner Blue, an endangered butterfly. She carefully releases it and hikes back through the flower-filled meadow surrounded by pines. A distant mountain, a solitary sentinel, provides a protective enclosure. Cool air and blue light slides down its side and flows toward her, washing her sins away so that she feels joy, if only for a little while.

Resting the net on her shoulder like a rifle, she wades in the grass enjoying the sweet fragrances of the wildflowers. Her red hair, wet with sweat, hangs in her face. She winces when she brushes it back. A raised patch on her scalp aches. Her father pulled her hair so hard this time her scalp separated from the bone and blood ran down to collect around her eyes. She has two black eyes. She told her teacher that she got them fighting, but the two stern ladies from the state showed up at the door again anyway.

Rosie brushes the tops of the wild grasses and flowers with her fingertips as she walks further into the meadow. Her boots swish in the grasses. This field is full of butterflies and she watches one fly high. Dark clouds crest the hills surrounding the meadow.

On her rainy walk home, her sweater covers a soft mesh box containing numerous captive butterflies. Her worn black work boots are muddy. Her bare, freckled legs poke out from her wet school dress. Thorns and twigs have left them scratched with dried blood. She is rangy and raw boned, not at all pretty, but beautiful in the twilight.

She opens her front door. Blue gray light flickers in the unlit room. It's the middle of May. She has missed dinner.

"Your school called again," her father says, glaring from the couch. "What the hell are you thinking? We called the police. They wanted to put out an Amber Alert, but since you do this all the God damned time..." He's dressed in his denim work shirt and brown Carhartt pants, his clothes from the slaughterhouse where he works. His sits with a filterless cigarette in his lips and a beer in his lap in front of the TV. Putting out the cigarette and standing, he spits a bit of tobacco from his tongue as Jack, her little brother, says, "Hi Rosie," and runs to her. She turns to Jack, but she can hear her father walking up behind her. He hits her in the back of the head, raking her with his knuckles. It hurts and she feels a chill inside her nose. She begins to cry.

"Derek, please don't," says her mother, coming in from the kitchen.

When he grabs Rosie by the hair, she feels something rip. She is led stumbling to her bedroom. Her mother watches with one hand holding her robe closed over her breasts and the other hand covering her mouth.

Rosie's off-white walls are hung with some of her grandmother's framed butterflies. Clothes, stuffed animals, a doll, and books spill from piles around her bed and across the floor. Dusty boxes containing mounted butterfly specimens line a table near the window. With a strong underhand, Rosie's father sends her stumbling onto the bed. He slips on a book and then kicks her things, his legs rising and stomping in a crazy goose step; a foolish marionette pulled by misunderstood strings. Pages float down through the air as he sends her books flying.

"You keep this room clean," her father shouts, clenching his tobacco stained teeth. He knocks over the table holding her grandmother's boxes of butterflies. Their papery wings crumble. Rosie sobs and covers her ears. He flings her dirty clothes everywhere, even onto the curtain rods. "If you don't keep this room clean, I'll throw this shit away and you can sleep on the floor ... And no more skipping school. You're only in fifth grade, God damn you." He slams the door. From her room, Rosie hears her parents arguing.

"Goddammit, he says, "I don't spend all day killin' cattle to come home to this bullshit."

"Your daughter's not a cow. You can't treat her like that."

"Shut the fuck up."

"You won't treat me like that either, asshole."

Rosie stands, stunned, in the middle of the room on an oval throw rug. Raindrops plink on the metal gutter outside the open window as she begins to clean up. She folds the clean clothes that were on her bed before being flung around the room. Mostly blue, her favorite color and mostly cotton, she doesn't like the way other fabrics feel on her skin. She gathers the books from the floor and replaces them on the shelves. She wants to please, to be neat. Her little brother dressed in his powder-blue pajamas with the feet in them brings her a cookie. An Oreo. He has brought cookies and a quart of milk in a carton.

"Are you ok?" Jack asks, handing her an Oreo.

"Yes."

They sit on the floor with the cookies, pull them apart and lick the centers one after another at the same time. She pulls her cookie apart and waits for him, brushing small crumbs from her lap with the back of her fingers. They take turns drinking milk from the carton getting brown cookie residue on the rim of the waxy fold out spout. Rosie has tears in her eyes but she smiles at Jack. The air from the window feels damp.

Rosie looks at the half-eaten Oreo package and asks, "Where did you get these? You didn't climb up on the counter again did you? Jack? I'm afraid you'll slip." She pats his pajama foot and then wipes her nose on her sleeve. "How was school today?"

"We planted seeds and we painted flowers like George Keef."

Rosie gives a few exaggerated nods. "Do you mean, Georgia O'Keefe?"

He takes a bit of cookie. "Yeah. She painted huge big flowers. Do you like painting?"

She sips from the carton and wipes her mouth with the back of her hand. "Yeah. What is your favorite thing at school?"

"Recess and PE."

"They have PE in kindergarten?"

Rosie looks around the trampled room.

Her grandmother had left behind five display boxes of preserved butterflies. She had given them to Rosie and Rosie treasured them. Four of them are lying shattered, the pieces scattered around the room with the fragile butterflies crushed into powder. One box survives the tempest. It holds her favorites, the Blues. When the cookies are gone, Rosie stands and steps over her brother's leg to hide the Blues box among her clean clothes in a drawer. Then, she and her brother finish cleaning her room.

A small-framed box with a mounted butterfly hangs crooked on her wall; it is about to fall. While Rosie works the nail back in place, her brother stands and gazes at it. It is a Morpho Blue from South America. Like Rosie, her grandmother loved butterflies. She had drawers and drawers of them arranged by species and regions. Rosie stands beside her brother and decides to make her own collection of butterflies like Grandma's.

"Can't you fix those?" Jack points at the pieces in the trash.

"No. I'm gonna make more. Some of my own." Rosie tousles his thick red hair and then gently spins him towards his own bedroom. "Come on," she says. "I'll tuck you in."

When Rosie's ready for bed, she pulls her butterflies from under her clothes in the drawer. With her fingertips, she pets the glass box like a holy reliquary of saints. In bed, she likes to imagine these butterflies coming to life as she sleeps, fluttering and soaring in the dark of her room, mating in flight, laying eggs on the torn pages of her books, the larvae eating the pages then crawling up a lamp and draping themselves from the shade to form chrysalids from which other butterflies fly forth singing songs of flowers and nectar among their friends.

She rolls over and adjusts her pillow so it won't bump the huge welt on her scalp. Her fingers tremble as she reaches up to touch her head. It stings.

In the morning Rosie sits up in bed, remembers her plan the night before, and gets to work on her collection. She pulls the rope that brings down the folding ladder to the attic. She whisks a cobweb from her face as she climbs to the silent room. From a small window near the roof, dust motes linger in a long shaft of light. The room smells musty. Grandma's old rocking chair, with the familiar squeak, waits in the corner. Rosie rocks in silence as she pushes down on the tip of the rocker with her toe. An old treadle sewing machine wedges in between the roof and the floor and an old trunk containing Grandma's valuable linens sits nearby. Rosie opens it and lifts some intricate lace and examines the needlework. There are boxes full of Grandma's science books. Rosie often reads books from the elementary school library, but she is still too young to read Grandma's books. Grandma was a scientist, but gave it up to raise Rosie's mom. Rosie sets the boxes of science books aside and opens another box. Inside are Grandma's handmade dresses and blouses. Moths had been at them, but Rosie admires the designs and would never throw them away. Someday she hopes to dress as beautifully as Grandma.

In a cedar chest, she finds journals among the woolens and an old tribal dress of ochre deer hide. It's very soft, almost like velvet. There are few decorations, just some cowrie shells circling its neckline. Rosie lifts the dress from the chest and finds another dress underneath it made of blue cloth and decorated with satin ribbons, porcupine quills, and cowrie shells in tight rows across the front and the back. Folded ribbons, as long as Rosie's arm, attach to the middle, hanging at regular intervals beginning below the cowrie shells and continuing to just above the bottom where a thick white ribbon lines the edge. Beneath the second dress is a bone-handled knife in a worn and stained fringed leather sheath. She lifts the knife and removes it from the sheath. She then slides the rusty knife into her boot. Looking around at the mess she made in the attic, she quickly returns Grandma's dresses to the chest.

Rosie picks up the journals. A few are handmade, one with beautiful leather binding of fish skin. She skims through the journals. There are sketches and photos, complete drawings, writings organized by date like a diary and then some that contain stories. One journal is mostly about Rosie. There are photos of her as an infant. Her smiling mother is holding Rosie wrapped in a pink blanket. Her father is looking over her mother's shoulder, also smiling and gazing at Rosie as if in love. Why does he seem to hate her now? She wishes she could make them happy.

Inside another journal, there are two photos of Rosie and Grandma standing amid thousands of butterflies in flight. In one, they both reach up as if to net them with their fingers. In the other, hundreds cover Rosie's body and hair while her grandmother laughs with her head thrown back. The butterflies are Monarchs.

The photograph was taken when Rosie was six. She and Grandma had flown to Mexico for a week to see the Monarch Butterfly Preserves. It was Rosie's first time riding on a plane and staying in a hotel. After a long drive up into the mountains, Rosie was surprised by millions of butterflies, weighing down the branches of the Oyamel trees. They flew like a river of wings. Rosie and Grandma were giddy when the butterflies began to settle and alight, covering them. Their guide had taken the photographs.

On the other side of the attic, she finds a box marked "butterfly stuff." Under an old pith helmet, Rosie finds a small hardbound book explaining the procedure for mounting butterflies, some jars, and a spreading board made of two strips of wood to pin the wings and allow the butterfly's thorax and abdomen to hang below the mounting surface.

Rosie takes the book. She rushes to her room to read it. When she finishes, she closes the book and sits with her eyes closed. Then she rereads a passage:

The killing jar is a plastic or glass container in which we will add few drops of Ethyl Acetate to asphyxiate the insect. At the bottom of the container is a tight-fit piece of upholstery foam that will absorb the poison drops and will protect the specimen from shock. A few drops can kill a dozen specimens. After the insects die, wait 10 minutes and transfer them in papered envelopes or other containers to preserve them in the best condition possible.

Rosie has a cylindrical butterfly cage made of soft net where she keeps her recently captured butterflies from the meadows. She prepares the jars and other things she needs for the procedure. She cleans off her little table and pulls up a chair. The butterflies are beautiful. She watches them for a while, then opens the cage and carefully removes an orange and brown skipper. "You are cute," she says, looking into his large dark eye. "I never really noticed." She lowers the little skipper into the killing jar and tightens the lid. An orange and brown powder coats her fingers.

The skipper buzzes around inside, landing on the side of the glass then flies around, banging itself over and over against the sides and making little tinks against the metal lid, before settling down on the bottom where it folds its wings and calms down, partially unfolding then refolding its wings. He takes a few steps on the bottom then stops. It moves its front foot, caressing the floor of the jar where the poison had been absorbed into the material. It makes a small attempt to fly again but only hovers an inch above the floor of the jar. It's as if an invisible rubber tether is pulling him back to the floor each time he takes wing. Rosie notices her breathing getting faster. She is feeling a little ill. The skipper's movements become smaller and farther apart in time. Rosie sits silently watching and waiting. After a long period with no movement, she taps on the glass with her finger and the skipper's legs collapse and he topples over dead. She wants to cry.

Opening the jar and removing the dead skipper, she looks at it very close. It reminds Rosie of a teddy bear with a furry face, big brown eyes, and stubby antennae. She touches his wings. The way the wings fold reminds her of paper airplanes. She feels guilty, like that time she pushed her little brother for not cleaning up his room. She had begun to yell at him, "You keep this room clean..." then heard herself saying the same thing her father said to her. She did not like the way that felt.

Instead of using the relaxing jar, which would be the next step in the mounting process, Rosie finds a little jewelry box that once held a cheap

Michael Newman

ring and places the dead skipper inside. She takes it and the live butterflies out into the garden where she buries it and releases the live ones, watching them flutter away in their awkward grace. She cries on her way inside. Her father sits on the couch in his work clothes with a long bloodstain running the length of his left leg. Rosie stares at him and then turns toward her mom and brother and explains that she is finished catching butterflies.

"I won't hurt them," Rosie says.

She places all of her gear in a big box and climbs up into the attic. She dumps the box in the corner and climbs back down to clean her room.

Rosie sits down at her table in her bedroom. An array of pastels spreads out like a rainbow. There is a large sheet of coarse textured paper with a pastel painting of a Luna Moth in progress. On the corner of the table, a large brown cocoon rests. On her walls are her handmade miniature butterfly replicas pinned as specimens and framed in Ryker specimen mounts. They are her little sculptures, her statues of saints.

She begins to work on the celadon greens in the wings of her painting. A spot on the wing requires a specific brown, a brown similar on the wings of the dead skipper. Holding the crayon between thumb and forefinger, she applies some color with small quick strokes and rubs the pigment into the paper with her middle finger. Orange brown residue stains her finger. When finished, she places the pastel painting in a drawer with several others of butterflies and moths.

As the school year nears its end, the class has been studying butterflies in science. Rosie has never worked so hard in school. On the last day before summer vacation, Rosie sits at her desk in the classroom and glances out the window at the hills that contain her butterfly meadow. She opens the window. A breeze flutters the curtains and carries away the stale odor of the room. Floating in a bumbling flight, a little blue butterfly, both beautiful and comic, enters through the open window. She holds her hand to the angelic little bug. The blue bobbles past, circles over the shiny black braids of another girl, and exits through the same window. As if the butterfly were a pied piper, Rosie climbs through the window, ignoring the protests from her startled teacher.

A small puff of wind lifts the butterfly high, Rosie follows across the playground toward the high chain link fences enclosing the school. Rosie stops a moment, then dashes forward and leaps onto the fence, climbing over. Dropping to the ground as her dress catches and rips, she looks back toward the teacher and classmates in the windows watching. The teacher is talking on a cell phone while climbing out the window herself. She then jogs toward Rosie, and the kids follow and begin to run too. Rosie smiles. The teacher calls to Rosie but Rosie locates the flying butterfly and chases it, her too-big blue dress flapping in the wind.

In dusty work boots and her blue shirt, torn from the chain link fence, she opens her front door. A light flickers in the unlit room. She has missed dinner again. Her father stands and glares at her. His hands are clenched and his teeth are clenched. Her mother grabs his arm. He turns slowly to his wife and hunches his shoulders, holding his arms out like a skinny ape, and stares her down.

Rosie's mother endures his glowering for a minute then wavers and drops her head.

Rosie walks to her room and waits for her father.

When he enters, Rosie says, "I won't do it again." Her father blinks as if unsure and then raises his finger.

"I won't do it again," she repeats and stands her ground.

He walks right up to Rosie and breathes on her; his breath smells like alcohol. He looks around at her neat and tidy room. He stares at the butterfly paintings on the wall. Rosie follows his gaze. Her mother comes into the room and puts her palm flat on his shoulder. She also looks at the paintings of the butterflies.

Her mother asks, "Did you make these, Rosie?"

Rosie nods.

"They are lovely."

Her father quickly suppresses the surprise on his face and then scowls as he runs his fingers through his hair. Rosie observes his behavior for a moment and then turns to her mother and says, "Thanks, Mom."

Rosie has the best summer of her short life. She spends a lot of time painting and drawing not just butterflies, but flowers, animals, a portrait of Jack and one of her Mom. The paintings make her happy and give her some confidence, but her life changing work is a painting of her father near the end of summer.

It is a straightforward attempt at a likeness, but it enrages him. He flies into a violent tantrum and grabs Rosie. When he seizes her hair and lifts her from her feet, she hears and feels tearing. She will look like a raccoon, again. He leads her by the hair like a reluctant dog into the corner and then backhands the top of her head, terrifying Jack and finally forcing her mother to run for the phone and dial 911. Her father is arrested. Rosie will not see him again for years. Later, her mother explains about the portrait that her father "hated himself and could not stand to see himself as you saw him."

It is fall and picture day at school. Rosie, a sixth grader, stands in line wearing her new dress. Divided at her waist, the top is blue with white polka dots and the bottom striped purple and brown. There is a little white collar that ties in a bow in front. She made it herself with her mother's help. On her feet, she wears her worn black work boots. As her turn approaches, she tidies herself up and her fingers touch the swollen spot on her scalp. The swelling is going down and it's not as painful to touch. The photographer points her to a stool. "Chin up, turn your head a little," he says, and when she is told to smile she does.

Returning to her classroom, she glances toward the hills and meadows where she spent so much time skipping school. She pauses. Her teacher, Mrs. Smith, is standing at the classroom door watching, alert. She calls, "Rosie ... Rosie," and as Rosie looks at her, Mrs. Smith waves her over.

"Come on Rosie ... Rosie, Come to class Rosie. Come to class, Rosie Jones."

Rosie jogs to Mrs. Smith and says, "What are we doing next, Mrs. Smith?"

"We are doing math, until recess, then your favorite subject, Art."

"But it isn't Friday."

"You looked so happy this morning that I decided to change things around."

"Thanks, Mrs. Smith"

"Are you going to make something for the Art contest?"

"Maybe. Can I make clothes for the contest? It's art too."

Mrs. Smith reaches down and places her hand on Rosie' cheek then touches her very short hair. "Who cut your hair?"

"I did. But then my mom fixed it."

"Why? Your hair was so beautiful, Rosie."

"I like my hair this way. So, can I? Make clothes for the contest?"

"You want to be the next Donna Karan, huh?"

"Who?"

Mrs. Smith grins. "I'll bring you some magazines. Did you make this dress all by yourself?"

"Mostly, I drew it and picked the fabric, and then my mom helped me sew it."

"How many dresses have you made?"

"Four so far. My mom said I can have my Grandma's old treadle machine if I don't skip class."

"Don't you like my class?" Mrs. Smith asks.

"Yes, I like it a lot."

"So, you won't skip?"

"No, I won't, I promise," Rosie says, "I don't really want to anymore anyway. So can I make clothes?"

"Sure you can, but I really would like to have a painting from you. I love your butterflies."

"Can I do both?"

"Yes," Mrs. Smith says.

They walk back to the classroom together and Rosie stops for a moment. "Can I sell my painting?"

"If you want, I might buy one myself ... Why?"

Rosie bounces up and down on her toes. "I want money."

"What for, sweetheart?"

"Painting and sewing stuff. Mom can't afford them very much now because Dad moved out."

"I heard about that. How are you doing with the change?"

"Good."

"Really?" She reaches out as if to touch Rosie's face but allows her hand to fall.

"Yep," Rosie says. "I don't like my dad."

Mrs. Smith looks long into Rosie's eyes. "Okay then," she says, "let's go inside" and watches as Rosie jogs into the room.

Rosie arrives home with her new school photos. She removes a sheet of small photos and cuts one out for herself, leaving the rest on the kitchen table. In her room at her desk, she opens the drawer where she keeps last year's picture. Her long red hair was braided like Grandma's and she was wearing her old faded blue sack dress, the one with holes, patched and un-patched, from climbing the fence and running in the meadows. Her eyes were black. "Coon eyes," the kids called her. She lays the new photo down next to the old one and compares. Her red hair is cropped close, her eyes are normal and she's wearing her new dress. The one she made with her favorite colors.

She props the photo up against her painting lamp, opens the killing jar, drops the old photo in, and screws on the lid.

Icarus, Falling
—after Matisse
by Paulann Petersen

The sky letting me plunge
without pause
clangs a blue of bells.
My wings tore off so long ago,
the raw swath across my shoulders
tries to scab. Each wing-piece
formed a star in the sky
so yellow, so huge
it hoards light. Wind skids
through my mouth and teeth.
Free-fall is the refrain I can't hustle
out of my brain. I lick
salt from my cracking lips.

My body's dark, the black
of ocean-bottom where I'll land.
I must learn to swallow light
before I can swallow the sea's water.
Those yellow stars made from my wings
learn to shine in daylight.
No way the heavens would turn
dark as me. In a black sky,
no one could note
where I begin and air ends.
Too few could see me fall.
Large as those birds I might touch
had I the time to reach out,
these stars flurry themselves aloft,
rising above me.

Who do I think I'm fooling?

Stars are set for life.
I'm not. It's me on the move,
not them. So far, I've named
only yellow and blue—
my black having gulped other colors.
There is a third. A stain. I wear
its blotch of red on my chest.
A stand-in for this plummeting heart.

Shared
by Ada Molinoff

He opens his arms, stands
still in the parking lot
at Dunkin' Donuts.
The girl trots to him,
he bends, she jumps,
he lifts her to his chest.

He holds her. They talk,
foreheads touching.

The woman brushes
her harried wisps of hair,
hands over the pink duffle.
She returns to her car,
waves. They won't look.

His weekend is
starting at five o'clock,
this Friday in March—
as good a time as any
to begin
again.

Right Here in Hollywood

by Jennifer Springsteen

Tammy and Dennis are on vacation. Dennis retired five years before from a security position at People First Credit Union in Texas. They've never been to the West Coast, but their daughter and her family moved to San Bernadino last year—even though the pay wasn't that much better than Brian could've got in Texas once you counted in cost of living—and they want to see the grandkids. Dennis figured it'd be nice to drive, and Tammy wanted to see Hollywood on the way.

Tammy and Dennis pull the truck off Highway 101 onto Hollywood Boulevard.

"What kind of skull collection?" Tammy asks with the Museum of Death brochure unfolded at eye level.

"Have to see." Dennis reaches under the dash and yanks the emergency brake. He takes his wallet from on top of the dash and rocks his butt to fit it in the back pocket of his dungarees. "All set?"

Tammy twists the rear view mirror and aims it at her mouth. She rolls her coral lipstick along her tiny lips. She blots with a tissue then puts the tissue and lipstick back in her pocketbook. "Ready," she says.

Inside, a young man sits behind the filmy glass in his ticket booth. There are two solid black plugs in his ears the size of quarters. They pay and walk through the black velvet curtains. Tammy says, "For the love of Pete, that boy made himself deformed."

"Wait till we get inside," Dennis tells her.

First they saw the artwork by serial murderers. "It just breaks my heart," Tammy says, "all that talent gone to waste."

They come upon a wooden electric chair.

"I can't believe our very own country would house this cruel, cruel machine. And we say the Nazi's were horrible." Tammy opens her palm at the display. "The stains. I mean the stains of sweat in the clothes of these men electrified. I just can't think about it." She says, "I'm so glad you left that prison and moved into private security services before they made you pull the lever."

Dennis has his hand folded behind his back. He's looking at a shriveled-up sponge.

Tammy tells him, "That's what they use on top of the heads so the hair won't catch fire." She points to the caption written on the display.

"I know," he says. He scratches the back of his neck like he does when he's ready for one of his speeches.

"What is it, Mr. Smartyface?" she asks. There's a Wrigley's in her purse and she rips it in half and gives him the bigger piece.

Dennis takes the gum and places the crumbled wrapper in Tammy's outstretched hand.

"I did it."

"Oh stop," she says.

He nods. "I did. I did it. I wet those sponges," he points to the display, "God bless it, I did."

It's silent in the museum and they hear the clip clop of feet somewhere and each other's chewing—Tammy with her mouth half open and Dennis with a whistle in his nose.

"Why didn't you tell me?"

Dennis shakes his head.

"Well, why are you telling me now?"

"Thought you should know."

Tammy's hands go to her hips, and she shifts to her left leg so her hip pokes out defiantly. "I didn't want to know."

"You do anyway."

Tammy walks into another dark room leaving Dennis there with the dried up sponge and fear-stained prisoner's clothes and the metal cuffs for the ankles and the big wooden chair that made men look like children. It wrapped them in its hard embrace and shook them loose. Rattled their teeth—yes, he'd seen that—the skin on their cheeks flapping and then the smell of urine. Cleaning up after. Not just the pee and the poo and the burning, but that other smell, something came undone inside them. Something spilled out hot and anxious.

Dennis finds Tammy in the next room with the shrunken skulls. Mounds of white, whisps of dark hair still attached to the crowns. He slips his hand into hers as easy as you please, and she lets him.

They stand together facing the empty sockets and hinged jaws.

"Wish you hadn't told me."

Jennifer Springsteen

"I know," he says.

The intercom lights up with a buzz. The voice of the young man in the booth spits surly and garbled. "Attention," he says, "the museum closes ..."

"What'd he say? When's it close? We just got here."

Tammy says, "I can't understand him. He's got one of those rods driven through his tongue."

"What haven't we been to?" Dennis holds the brochure to his face. Squints.

"There's car crashes some place." Tammy looks past the shrunken skulls to the souvenirs of serial killers.

"I'm ready to go if you are," Dennis says. He's thinking of the electric chair. He's thinking he's hungry and his feet are starting to ache.

"I'm going to the basement," she tells him. "They took our ten dollars, and I'm going to get my money's worth."

In the basement, they stand before exhumed bodies under glass coffins. Tammy frowns, bends over a coffin. "Why'd they say they dug these poor people up?"

"Says here they donated their bodies to science. They used them to learn forensics."

Tammy stands again and moves to the next case. "See there? That's why I refuse to donate my body to science. You think you're going to save some ailing child with a kidney transplant and you wind up cut apart and buried naked."

"It's still in the name of science."

"You won't catch me naked in one of these museums."

Dennis says, "No, I reckon I won't."

After looking at all the coffins, (at the last one Tammy says, "You can't even make out if it's a man or a woman. It could be an animal for all we can tell.") Dennis says, "We should go back up."

But Tammy doesn't want to. She wants to get her money's worth and to punish Dennis for keeping that secret from her all these years. Who keeps a thing like that from his wife, she'd like to know. But after she satisfies herself looking at the blown up photos of people who'd been attacked by animals and survived, she makes her way back to the main hall and up the basement stairs. Dennis follows her up, says nothing.

It's dark upstairs. There are no lights on in the display cases at all. There are just the tiny floor lights as small as Christmas tree lights crudely stapled at intervals along the hallway floors.

"Oh no," Dennis says.

"What?" asks Tammy, "Oh no, what?" But she knows what. She follows Dennis to the front ticket booth and there it sits, a big empty pill bottle. Dennis walks to the front doors and gives them a pull. Nothing. Then he goes back to the booth and tries that door, too. Locked tight.

"Well, I'll be gall durned," he says.

Tammy's mouth opens. The strap of her purse has fallen from her sloped shoulder and digs in right above her elbow. The skin underneath it is puffed and rubbed red. "We're trapped," she says looking right at Dennis. Like he'd done it.

Dennis checks the hole in the ticket booth to see if his arm can get in where the money and tickets slide back and forth. Maybe he can reach the phone. He shoves it in up to his forearm and it sticks, but he keeps it there on the other side of the glass, wiggling his fingers toward the phone. Finally he pulls it back out. "Should've gotten a cellular phone like Meg and Booger told us to."

"Don't call him that."

"Well, unless there's some night watchman coming in ..."

Tammy turns to the front doors and slams them with her palms. Her purse jerks back and forth in the crook of her elbow. "We're trapped in here! Help us, we're trapped!"

Dennis comes from behind and stops her hands with his and then turns her around for a hug. He feels her heart racing on his chest and the shiver in her arms. "I don't want to be stuck here," she says.

"I know it," Dennis says. "These places must have night watchmen. There's thieves everywhere." He pulls his arms from her and points to the floor by the far wall. "Let's sit."

"I can't."

"Well, you should." He gets there in three long strides, puts his back to the wall, lets his knees bend, and slides down.

Tammy walks over, stands in front of him for a minute. Her purse strap is in her grip now, and it sways at her calf. Finally she drops it and leans at the waist to place her hands on the floor. On all fours, she scootches her wide bottom around and flops her legs out before her. All this with huffing and moaning and little annoyed grunts.

Dennis pats her thigh. "Better?"

Jennifer Springsteen 61

She shakes her head. He can see her front teeth on her lip, trying to keep from crying. So he pats again.

After a time, she says, "Why didn't you tell me about the prison? About what you did?"

Dennis takes his hand from her thigh. Right down the hall is that contraption. Those stained clothes. He's stuck here with them. With Tammy condemning him. "We needed the money," he says. She stays quiet so he keeps going. "It was right after Booger was born. Meg was in diapers, and we needed a bigger place and food on the table. We needed the money."

"You said you got a raise."

"I did."

She looks at him for a while thinking of how else to argue. He feels her eyes on him, warming his forehead. Agitating. She straightens the bottom of her blouse and picks the fuzzies off her pants. She sniffs and says, "All these years, and I don't even know you."

"I'm what I always was. Including what I done. What you don't know's yourself."

Tammy's lips quiver, and right away she's crying. "What's that supposed to mean, I don't know myself."

Dennis is even-keeled, but she's getting to him, that's plain to see. He crosses his arms across his thin chest and crosses his feet at the ankles, too. "Perfectly fine to go gawking at all the nastiness in life long's you don't get your own hands dirty."

For her turn, Tammy hefts up her purse and shoves it in her lap. Wraps her arms around it. "I don't believe you just said that."

He waves his hand. "Look at this place."

The frame securing how they've pictured their lives moves off center. It doesn't obscure what's there, but the hold feels different. These shifts have happened before. Like when she accused him of sleeping with her best friend, Leslie Anne, or the miscarriage, or when they almost lost the house, or when Booger, God bless him, went to jail for selling marijuana, the shadow in Dennis' lung. All of it tangled together with forty years lying in the same bed smelling each other's farts and morning breath.

"I forgive you," she says. Kinda quiet.

Dennis takes in a long breath and lets it out low and loud. He keeps his eyes straight ahead, right at the ticket booth. "Woman," he tells her, "I don't need your forgiveness."

When he turns to face her, her mouth is wide open.

He softens. "If you'd seen what these men done, Tammy. Things to children. To women. To animals."

She shakes her head, says, "If I'd known."

"You'd what?" Dennis won't let her out of his gaze.

"I don't know. I'd..." She opens her purse and shoves her hand in up to the elbow. Comes out with gum. She's violent with the paper and this time takes the whole piece, doesn't offer Dennis any.

She chomps for a while looking off to her right. "Maybe we could of just talked about it some. Talked about something aside from diapers and spit up."

Dennis pats her thigh again. "New mamas don't want to hear about murderers."

"Sometimes I thought about becoming one," she says and they laugh in the easy way they do, rubbing away at the raw edges. Their backs are bent, and they stare at their shoes. Dennis' white tennis shoes, Tammy's brown clogs. They focus on what is solid, knowable. These simple things they understand about each other.

Tammy pulls at the underarms of her blouse and fans her face with her thin hand. "Maybe they turned the AC off, " she says. Dennis looks around for some evidence of that and tugs at his collar.

She asks, "Were you scared?"

"Of the men?"

"No. Of watching it. Doing it."

"Yeah."

"Did it make you feel powerful? Like God or somebody."

Dennis shakes his head hard. "No. The whole thing feels weak. Even the family behind the glass cries. Watching a grown man get killed like that."

"But some people like things like that. Public hangings and things."

"I reckon so."

Tammy's ashamed of herself for how excited she'd been about coming to the museum, about that brochure she found at the hotel and said, "Lets go, it'll be fun."

Dennis takes her hand in his. "I don't like to think about it much."

"Okay."

"I can still see them sometimes. I hear the water running from the sponge and them calling out."

"Are you scared you're going to hell?"

Dennis turns away from her. "Not scared of hell, I'm just tired of thinking about them all the time. Smelling them."

There are voices on the other side of the big doors and the lock twists in its shell. It bumps and clunks and finally pushes in with the bright California sun at it's back. The boy with the earplugs stands blinking in. A skinny girl curves like an S beside him, holding his arm.

"Oh, shit," he says when he steps in and sees Tammy and Dennis on the floor. "You two okay?"

Dennis gets up first and reaches out his hand to Tammy.

The boy goes on, "I remembered you two coming in late, and I didn't see you leave. I was on the bus when I realized."

The girl nods. "I drove him back here to check. I hate coming to this place," she says, "gives me the creeps."

On her feet, Tammy walks towards the boy. "How could you do that?" she asks him.

He looks at the girl, embarrassed. "I just closed up. I forgot you came in. I sent a ten minute warning on the loud speaker."

Tammy waves her hand. Shakes her head no. She puts her boney fingers to her own ears—each white lobe host to a silver teardrop shot through with deep blue turquoise. "I mean your ears. How can you do that to yourself? Does your mom know?"

The girl titters, bites her bottom lip. She keeps both her arms wrapped around one of his. The boy is nervous. He shifts his weight from one sneaker to the next. "She doesn't like them," he says.

"They never grow back," the girl says. He gives her a look.

"I can't understand it," Tammy says, "a perfectly handsome face gone to ruin."

He goes pink and the girl laughs, covering her mouth with her palm.

Dennis holds his arm out for Tammy and looks at the boy. "Can we go now?"

The boy apologizes again and shakes free from the girl to let them pass. Once they've gone through the door, he steps out with them. "I'm sorry," the boy says, "I really am."

Dennis reaches out for the boy's shoulder, "I know you are, son."

Dennis and Tammy walk back to the hotel without saying anything else to each other. They're both looking around, thinking, Hollywood. In the lobby of the hotel, they stop at the brochure kiosk and flip around for some place to eat. Tammy takes a brochure and reads it out to Dennis on the way to the room, "Hollywood Christ Church," she says. "They have services tomorrow at 8:15 and 11:15. We should go, Dennis, right after our continental breakfast."

Dennis tosses the key card on the vanity and lies down on the made-up bed with his shoes on and everything. He puts his arms behind his head and closes his eyes. Tammy climbs up in her stocking feet, releases the pillow from its tight fold, and puts it under her armpit. She's looking at his closed face. He knows it and smiles. "What are you smiling for?" she asks. She swats his arm with the church brochure. Dennis gets the giggles and then Tammy does, too. She lays her head on his chest and spreads her hand across his stomach. She can hear all the squeaks and gurgles in there. And the low droning pump of his gentle heart.

The Fasting Month
by Amy Miller

I haven't asked the details,
whether it's dawn to dusk
like Ramadan, or a perfect
circle of hunger. Surely

you drink, surely you've learned
of water's grim preeminence.
You've lost substance and heft,
as if you've shed yourself

of gravity's dull domain
and floated up, found yourself
lodged serenely in a branch,
looking down. You've dwindled

to something nearly
dangerous, a wavering staff
of the essentials. Even that
could be more basic,

your soul subtracting
and subtracting
until you've folded
one too many times

and disappeared
completely.

Falls Along the McKenzie
by Julia Kolchinsky Dasbach

I thrust my hands
into Sahalie's melting throat.
Before I could bring

the liquid to my lips,
it became a game
of whose skin

could outlast whose.
His voice began: *One, two, three*—
the current throbbing

cobalt cold against my palms.
It would have been
so easy then, to give in

to its pulse, letting fingers
sink a little deeper
beyond this place

where water whitens—
the man beside me
only a hollow drum,

echoing the crash
on sharpened rocks:
Eleven, twelve, thirteen.

Would he hear my body
fall into the flow or think
it was the thawing snow

coming away with moss
and mountain, turning
the waters a deeper blue?

Twenty-one, twenty-two—
It was so tempting then
to let our lifelines wash away

with cascade's rush,
to imagine my heart
submerged in ice-tide, first

accelerate ahead, then
slow to the stillness
that once bore

its beating, raging pace
he watched above.
Thirty-three, thirty-four—

my hands lost feeling
in the water, grew heavy.
How long would Sahalie

need to carry me inside
before I'd rise
quiet, clean, and empty?

Rise, like the driftwood trunk
he mistook for the skeleton
of a beached whale, a beast

outlasting the both of us.

Bodies Like Weeds
by Matt Young

O ur base was at an old Iraqi vacation spot named Baharia. All these little clay and stucco one and two-bedroom huts circled a man-made lake. On our rest and refit days our lieutenant would lead us in motivation runs around the entire perimeter, about four miles. It wasn't so bad at first. But then the winter began to dwindle. Running it during the summer was an ass-kicker. The asphalt got so hot it was like running in peanut butter. Trucking around a man-made lake in one-hundred fifteen degree weather, trying to echo cadence, surrounded by miniature date palms and concrete and steaming macadam in the middle of a damned war, we felt like maybe we should rub a little sunscreen on our noses, maybe pop into the water for a dip.

But the goddamned water was off-limits.

As the summer heated up, it became harder and harder for the higher-ups to keep all us enlisted guys out of the lake. If a guy got caught taking a soak they might make him police call trash around our compound. When that didn't work, they forced extra guard duty on our off days. Finally, they started in with the non-judicial punishment and removal of rank.

None of it worked.

One of the more senior officers finally let it get out that on the island in the center of the lake, which was connected by bridge to the peninsula that provided a home for the base's phone center, a three story house had once stood. They told us it had belonged to a prominent Ba'ath party member, and when he would go there on holiday he would call for women, girls really, from the local villages. They told us he had a whole harem of kidnapped girls.

When he was done with them, he would strangle them or torture them or just shoot them in the head. Then he'd have their bodies tossed off the concrete dock, into the lake.

None of us knew if it was true.

What really made us wonder were the eels. At dusk during the summer we would see these five and six foot long fresh-water eels come to the surface to feed on the swarms of mosquitoes. We all wondered how they could get so big just from eating the little insects.

They must've been down there eating something else.

A cross-sectioned husk had since replaced the manse. Bombed out with five hundred pounders and MOABs and whatever else those Air Force boys could throw on it. The rubble reached across the bridge, leaving huge hunks of rebar laden concrete on the call center side.

The call center peninsula was no more than fifty meters from our clay hut doorstep, as the crow flies, right under our noses. But to walk all the way was at least three miles. The time difference in the States was around eight hours. We had to call at night; it was the only way to get hold of our girls, which wasn't a big deal. Not at first.

But a few months in, all the married guys and guys with girlfriends started thinking about what was going on back home. Why hadn't I gotten a letter yet? Where was that package she promised? Why didn't she answer the phone? What did she do at night? On the weekends? Who was she hanging around with? Eight thousand miles of distance could put a relationship in a dark place.

To add to it all, there was nothing to do in the damned place on our days off except go to a little gym with weights that guys made from tent poles and sandbags. Or jerk off. But there was only so much weight you can hold up, and only so many women you could fantasize about until you hurt yourself. So we'd wait around, go to the gym or whatever else, until nightfall when we could make the call in hopes someone would answer and put our suspicions to rest.

To pass the time, Jackie Wales and I built a raft.

It was four, maybe five months in. Anyway, Jackie and I got the idea from a movie. Some western. We thought we would build the raft and then run a skinny line of parachute cord from our bank to the call center peninsula's bank, next to the bridge leading to the old estate. That way we wouldn't have to walk.

Jackie didn't believe in ghost stories, he figured the higher-ups were just blowing smoke. I dipped in and fed off his confidence, but I still couldn't go near the water at dusk. All those fat, slick-bodied eels skimming the surface, trying to fill up on tiny bugs. And the way they swam, in a circular search pattern, made me think they were looking for something else.

We passed the next few weeks collecting the pieces we needed from trash heaps and the motor pool. Jackie started us out; he found a piece of plywood about five feet by seven feet that had been tossed onto the unlit part of a burn pit. In between security patrols or teaching the new-joins, Jackie and I worked. We designed the raft to have two long arms coming off the sides so we would have extra stability, seeing as we were both pretty big guys, and didn't want that thing to go under once we got it on the water. We drilled holes in the plywood board for lashing humvee inner tubes. The thing was a damned work of art.

During that second week of construction I got a package during mail call. A friend of mine in the States had sent me some whiskey in a plastic apple juice container. No kidding, the guy bought one of those feeder syringes used to wean puppies. He attached a fourteen-gauge needle to it, and syringe-by-syringe moved the whiskey into the bottle. When he was done he heated up a lighter and melted the hole shut. Just in case the guys at customs decided they wanted to open my package, he told me later.

So anyway, I had the bottle of whiskey, and Jackie and I, we were almost done with the raft. We needed one more inner tube. I told our sergeant I would look after the new-joins. Teach them something; keep up appearances for the higher-ups. So Jackie said he would get the tube. The motor pool was on the other side of base, away from the lake, about five miles. He would be gone most of the day.

It worked out.

Our maiden voyage was to be that night. I figured I'd bring the whiskey and we could celebrate; break the champagne as it were.

By the time Jackie got back from the motor pool, rolling the inner tube in front of him like some damned Andy Griffith character, whistling and ditty-bopping down the street, I was in a sour mood. I didn't get anything from my girl during mail call, hadn't in fact in about a month and a half. I'd written when we'd first arrived, before the rumors started, about the lake, how beautiful it was, how it looked like something out of a travel ad for Florida. I couldn't believe I hadn't heard back, like she didn't have the goddamned time. We talked on the phone once or twice a week, if I could get there, but the conversations were always short, she'd always start crying and then I just couldn't take it and I'd have to hang up.

So I wanted some whiskey, I wanted it bad. And I wanted to give my girl a call and really chew her out, make her feel as low as I did. This time I wasn't going to hang up. I wanted to listen to her cry, sobbing her eyes out on the other end of the line. I thought it might make me feel better.

Jackie was still in a fine mood; he'd spent all day shooting the shit with a buddy of ours that worked down at the motor pool. We all called him Big John-T because no one could pronounce his last name. The guy was salty for sure. He was on his third pump to the sandbox in as many years. We all wanted him to work on our trucks. He did the things you usually had to grease a guy for: attaching extra spotlights, building spare tires. It was all stuff we could do ourselves, you know, but who wanted to? We hooked him up with smokes and the occasional skin mag when we could get our hands on it. It was more like a gift, than greasing the guy really. He wasn't some bastard who tried to jam us up for a carton of stateside smokes for running a switch line. Anyway, he was good company at least.

So Jackie just wanted to relax, have a smoke, eat some chow, and hit the rack. He sat on an old box of MRE's. "Come on," he said, "let's go to chow. I heard they got Salisbury steak tonight."

"No, goddammit. Let's get this thing done with. The sooner we get done with it the easier everything will be," I told him.

"But, I'm hungry. Salisbury steak night's only once a month." He dropped his head between his knees and let his shoulders sag.

"Jesus, Jackie. Salisbury steak, Salisbury steak. Don't you think your girl wants you to call her? Here you are, worried about Salisbury steak, and your girl's all the way back home wondering if you're alive," I said, putting my hand on his shoulder. He looked up at me and smiled.

"Tina knows I'm alright. I send her a letter every day."

It was true. I'd seen him do it. Every damn day, he wrote that girl a letter. I always wondered what in hell could he have so much to write about.

"But you're right. She sure would like to hear my voice," Jackie said.

So we set to finishing.

Lashing the last tube on to the other arm took about ten minutes to make sure the tube wouldn't roll, and the knots were good. We did our work between a few of the huts where our humvees were parked. I cut the last tail hanging from our square lashing, with my knife. I carried a knife on me all the time back then, like a kid with a stuffed animal.

Jackie carried letters from his wife. Other guys carried rosaries or wore a crucifix or Star of David. I just happened to carry a knife. The thing even went to bed with me under my pillow.

The longest part was waiting for dark. We smoked cigarettes and watched the sun come down over the lake. The sunsets there were like nothing I'd ever seen. This burning orange ball of a sun silhouetted the date palms, and I found myself thinking what the place must've looked like thirty or forty years back.

I could imagine families swimming and laughing, young couples eating picnics. I smelled cooking meat and sweat and suntan oil. I thought how good that water would feel in the summer when the needle pushed one-twenty. I watched girls surfacing from the cool blue water to warm themselves in the throbbing sun. My girl and I were there, sunning ourselves on the latticed decorative concrete shore, loving one another, never having to worry about eight thousand miles or how or when to make a phone call or who was the last to send a letter.

Then it was dark, and those people, those feelings, those smells, they went right away along with the light, back down to the bottom of the lake. Back down to the bottom with all those dead rotting girls, and the eels. I felt my chest tighten as frigid air settled inside me.

The raft wasn't so much heavy as awkward, and what made it worse was the bottle of whiskey in my cargo pocket. The plastic kept slapping my knee, and the sloshing sounded like artillery going off over the water. We had to carry the raft above our heads, but when it gets dark in the desert, it gets pitch, so we weren't worried about being seen.

We didn't have any paddle, and we needed to scull across the first time to lay the line. So we wrapped duct tape around the business end of a broom and made our own.

The raft made a horrible splash when we dropped it in the water and we sat there crouched next to the lake, waiting. I could hear Jackie's heartbeat, swear to God, just as plain as if he were talking to me. The coolness of the night showed our breath rising all around us like it was trying to get away, away with those families and women, into the warmth. But we didn't hear anything after that splash.

Jackie was heavier, so I had to go first. I tied one end of a cord to a stout palm, took the oar, and stepped onto the raft. It stayed afloat. Jackie pushed it out a bit, then leapt from shore about three or so feet. He didn't make a sound. I couldn't believe how he just glided right on top of that plywood like a cat jumping to a windowsill.

I remember being happy then. It was a strange feeling. Being in a shitty situation, separated from everything, wondering whether or not some guy in some bar somewhere was hitting on my girl, but still feeling happy. It made me ashamed. I tried to imagine being a civilian and having some veteran tell me they were happy while they were at war. I thought they'd probably throw me in some nuthouse and lose the key.

Laying the cord was easy. I paddled us across halfway while Jackie spooled the line, then we switched. We were two braves on a raiding party paddling a canoe into enemy territory. It felt like being kids again.

On the other side we secured the cord to a huge piece of blasted concrete. The line was slack enough that it would lay in the water during the day, invisible unless someone walked down to the bank. Since it was just our boys on the other side, and no one lived on the call center side, we figured we were home free.

The shoreline of the lake was sloped concrete, so the raft wouldn't silhouette itself. No one walking outside, or having a smoke at the call center could see the winged shape. It must've been ten or eleven o'clock then, and we both decided to make a call. I left the bottle there so it wouldn't bulge in my pocket, and the bastard working the call center wouldn't get suspicious.

I waited in line and got called up before Jackie. I sat there and dialed, and listened as the phone rang to my girl's recorded message. I sat for the full twenty minutes they allow, just calling over and over. She never answered.

"Hey," I said to the kid working the call center. "What the hell's the idea? I just used up half my damn calling card trying to get hold of my girl. What kind of scam you trying run?"

"Maybe she didn't hear it ring?" suggested the kid.

"Bullshit. My girl would answer if the phones were working like they were supposed to," I said. The kid shrugged and waved his arm at everyone else having conversations around the room. I walked outside for a smoke, and waited for Jackie.

In the chilled summer air I thought when we got back to our hut, I'd write my girl a letter. Write her and tell her I'd tried to call; I'd write about how all I wanted to do was talk to her; about how she was all I thought about; how without her, coming home seemed pointless.

I stood there, waiting and smoking and thinking and the more I thought about her at home in her warm bed, eating good food, hitting the snooze on the alarm clock and the silence button on her cell phone, doing whatever the hell she wanted, the more heated I got. I started thinking who the hell she thought she was. I knew she must be off work. Christ it was early morning there; she should answer the phone. Was she in bed, in our bed with some other guy, some chump we went to high school with who had never done a damn thing?

My mind made it true. He probably worked at the GM plant outside town, and they had met at Pike's bar, where she went after work with her girlfriends. He offered to buy her a drink and she said no at first. She had a few more drinks with her girlfriends, and when she went to cash out he was still there. He pulled out a stool for her, ordered her a drink, her friends left, and she sat down. She told him about her fiancé in Iraq, how he wouldn't be home for another four months.

"It just gets lonely around the house when I'm not working," she said.

He told her that was too bad, that he would never leave her behind. Then she was underneath him while the two of them went at it, huffing and panting, sweating in the warmth of our sheets on our mattress in our bedroom in our house, while I sat out in the cold by a lake full of the dead. I knew it then, I knew it just like I knew my own goddamned face.

I wanted to hit her, really give it to her, wrap my fingers around her neck, and let her know what it felt like to be cold and alone. Maybe when I wrote her, I'd write about the mansion, and what happened to the women there. Maybe I'd tell her about the eels.

Then, out walked Jackie, happier than ever, with that little goddamn bounce in his step.

"Tina sent some nudie pictures a couple weeks ago," he said, and started to giggle. I wished I had Jackie's girl.

I told him he could have all my drink if he let me see those pictures and we laughed. Jackie laughed for real.

We loaded the raft the same way as before, but I made sure to have hold of the line this time. We pulled the cord, gliding through nothingness. We stopped at what we thought was the center point between banks, and goddamned if I hadn't forgotten the paddle. Jackie took a tight hold on the line. We didn't want to lose it and float into the dark.

I pulled the bottle from my trouser pocket and broke the plastic seal. That charcoal sweet whiskey smell sent my mouth watering, and I took a great grimacing pull. I remember thinking that I would retch when the heat hit my belly, and I covered my mouth with my forearm and handed the bottle in Jackie's direction. We lay down after a few drinks, with the roughness of the plywood against our clothes, and liquor warmth spreading through our guts. We looked up at the stars.

I asked him about Big John-T, and he set in with this story John-T had told him.

"John-T said after they took Baghdad in oh-three that a buddy of his ran a convoy to Baharia," Jackie said. "They were running higher-ups all around for meetings or somewhat like that. He said that when his buddy got there, the Army was dragging the lake, tossing huge lengths of chain and hooks over-board these barges."

"So?" I asked.

"John-T's friend sat there and watched them until they pulled the chains in, and damned if it wasn't bodies they were pulling out of the lake, all around the bombed out house at the tip of the peninsula," Jackie said.

I was quiet then, I was dead quiet, and sober. I felt all that whiskey burn out of my system. I knew that it was true, all of it, and I didn't want to be on the raft anymore, God I couldn't stand it. I kept thinking about pale slimy dead flesh, sloughing off the bone, empty eye sockets staring up at the bottom of our small square of safety, jealous of our life. I thought of them down there, bloated, and swaying like weeds in the slight current from the aquifers that fed the lake. I imagined the eels gorging themselves on whatever they could loosen with their dull teeth.

I grabbed for the line, which surprised Jackie into letting the cord go loose into the dark. There was a pathetic sound as the line hit water. We stared at one another through the blackness, knowing everything was true. We sat there, stranded with the dead.

We got up on our knees to look out into the night and try to see how far from shore we were, if we were drifting or not. The dark was so absolute it was hard to tell. It felt at once as though we were spinning through nothingness out of control, and like we were cemented in the same place where the line had gone in.

"I don't think we've moved, do you?" Jackie asked.

"I can't tell," I said. "It's too dark." I shut my eyelids and opened them. There was no difference in what I saw, except when I shut my eyes I could still see my hands wrapping around my girl's throat. I could feel the spittle from her lips hit my face as she choked on her last breath. The splash of the water resounded in my ears as I dropped her from the concrete dock, with the decrepit mansion in the background. I watched her float into the depthless water, eels encasing her corpse as it sunk out of view.

"I'm going to reach in and see if maybe it didn't sink," Jackie's voice opened my eyes.

"Jesus," I said. The rustling of Jackie rolling up his sleeves and scraping his knees across the plywood overtook the night.

"Help me here, would you?" he asked. "Just make sure I don't fall into this shit."

"Jesus," I said again, taking him around the waist. I thought I could hear the eels sliding over the water in the distance. For sure they could smell the living skin, the oils it gave off, as soon as it touched the water. They would take Jackie, they would take him and I wouldn't be able to do a goddamn thing about it.

"Got it," he said. I could tell he was smiling.

We pulled back to shore, and all I could think of were all those dead girls down there in the dark, my girl swaying with them, and I thought I might start to cry. Jackie went right to sleep that night. He and the four other men we shared a hut with slept. I listened to the sounds of their sleep for I don't know how long. Until I couldn't take it anymore.

I stood outside the door staring into the nothing in the direction of the still water. It felt like being caught in a trance. I checked my watch; it was four in the morning. Then I walked it, all the way to the peninsula, right before the bridge where we tied the parachute cord.

I didn't take my eyes off that water the entire time.

Then, there I was at the concrete boulder. That piece of rock had once been apart of the mansion. Maybe it was part of the man's floor, he could have walked on it. His bathtub or his bed or his goddamned refrigerator could have covered it.

I stayed as far as I could from the glassy surface of the lake. I mean I was hugging that damn chunk of concrete. I cut the line without letting the water out of my sight.

After the three miles back, I laid awake the rest of the night, I couldn't close my eyes without seeing my girl's decaying face, eyeless, swaying, rooted to the bottom of the lake.

A few days later, Jackie asked me if I wanted to go to make a call. I brought what was left of the whiskey and we headed to the shore. We had hid the raft under some palm fronds and dried weeds. Along with the pitched shoreline, it was perfectly camouflaged.

We uncovered the raft, and then Jackie tugged the line, but he pulled and kept pulling.

We sat and cursed the one who had done it. I told him someone had probably spotted the oar I'd left, and seen the line hanging in the water on the other side. I could feel his frustration, hell, he was damn mad. I hunkered down on my haunches, not feeling a bit guilty, pulled out my smokes and the bottle and offered both to him, putting him in a considerably better mood.

We walked up the embankment and stood on the road, letting our heads swim in the rest of the booze.

"You want to start walking?" Jackie asked me.

"You go on ahead, I think I'll stay here," I said.

After Jackie had disappeared around the curve I pulled a crumpled letter from my pocket. It came earlier in the week, and I'd been carrying it and reading it ever since. It was a Dear John. She'd left me, not for anyone else, she wrote. Just can't handle it, she wrote. Put your things in storage, she wrote. She wrote she was sorry, she'd written it more than ten times throughout the entire thing.

The end wasn't a goodbye, instead she wrote the lake sounded nice and she was happy to know I was in a safe place away from bad things. I read that part over and over until I convinced myself it was the truth.

Aloha Oregon
by Ken Embery

It was a spectacular spring morning.
The sun was just up over South Maui.
The air was still and cool,
And the voices of the apapane and kiwikiu called and
Echoed,
High and far away in the palm forest,
And waves, fine big waves, slammed into Makena.
The thunder of it grew as I hiked from the blacktop parking lot,
Through narrow openings in the vehicle barrier of low cement pillars and
thick steel cable,
Down onto the sand access trail and then winding along the trail,
Through the tunneled shade of the palm forest,
Toward the lightning and diamond blue blaze of ocean,
Eager to throw my body at
       the
         falling
            slabs
       and
ride
  up
       the
         spinning
              faces
                  of
         opposite
    moon.
But suddenly,
I realized
Again,
My wife is not with me.
Her dust dances with mechanical pirates above Walt's slow rippled canal and

A handful of Julie grinds sole foot the highest landing of the tallest slide at
Blizzard Beach and
She lies, nurturing, rich California soil burst red, white, yellow, striped
Flowers in profusion;
In gardens;
In vast, famous, Big Ear's and Cinderella gardens,
Gardening, my how she loved to garden and to Disneyland and to serve her
children up smiles.
And for seven steps,
Seven steps exactly,
I held it off; Viking proud to have flown the curved horizons forth and
back, forth and back,
With the kids snuggled close and
Cradling the Shanghai urn in my right arm in my left arm in my right arm in
my left.
Please put that in the overhead, sir.
No.
Came the eighth step,
Graveyard shifters, eyes bloodshot desperate for sleep,
Stood in the palm shade, blasting recycled stink from brick worn, faded
green, rubber fragrant hoses;
Washing my Jules into the grates of conglomerate gutters.
This nasty, certain vision stopped me like a
Playground gut punch until
My angel of the earth leaned near and whispered,
Don't be such a coward.
Take the next step.
I smiled to remember that
This kind, funny nurse, who'd eased ten thousand sufferings,
Was tough as nails.
And I took the next step, and the next,
And I caught many good waves before breakfast,
With the whales breeching and spouting nearby in the sunny, ungodly blue
channel.

Triplane
by Geronimo G. Tagatac

I stood across the street from the America First Mortgage Company building on the morning after Ann died and waited for her to show up for work. I couldn't bear the thought of her not being able to understand why her friend, Marsha, the receptionist, would fail to look up and say good morning and why Mark, her supervisor, had taken the things out of her desk and put them into a cardboard box. I was waiting for my dead wife to come striding up the sidewalk the way I'd first seen her, five years ago. When she did, I'd run across the street and catch her before she could enter the building, put my arms around her waist and pull her to me and inhale the aroma of her short hair. We'd walk up Chemeketa Street, to the Minam Café where we'd order coffee and pancakes with maple syrup and I'd explain to her that there was no need for her to go to the office on this or any other morning.

At eight o'clock, I took my cell phone out and called work. Then I told my manager about what had happened. I did it in as few sentences as I could. Unexplained fatigue, an exam, emergency heart surgery. The sudden, post-surgical, downward direction in all of Ann's vital signs and her death at two in the morning. Yes, I think I'll take a week off, I said. I folded my cell phone and dropped it like a stone into my pocket.

Up the street, where Ann should have been, came a woman pushing a shopping cart. I stared at the woman with her weathered face and stringy blond hair, shoving her overloaded cart, its left front wobbling and rattling. Suddenly, I wanted to scream, "Get the hell off of the street! You, with your stringy blond hair and your hard-life face will never take her place!" But I just stood silently and watched the shopping cart woman rattle past me, her watery blue eyes anchored to something. As she went by, she whispered, "I know you."

Crazy old loon, I thought.

After Ann's funeral, the numbness that descended on me shut out all of the high frequency sounds in my life. Unable to hear the beep of the microwave, my food went cold. The music from the stereo and my TV became an undifferentiated hum that blended with the sound of the refrigerator to produce a background noise that made everything blurred. It was a narcotic sound that filled the whole house and slowed my every move to half speed.

To escape it, I began waking before dawn and walking the empty streets. Only the light, early fall rain kept me company, which was good. I had no wish to run into anyone I knew, to look into their tight faces and eyes and to listen to their sympathetic words. I didn't want to explain anything to the ones who hadn't heard. And ten minutes after my return, I could recall nothing of what I had seen. The only evidence of my walk was the dampness of my clothes and shoes, and heaviness in the muscles of my thighs and calves. A sympathy card arrived in the mail, signed by my co-workers. After that, I put all of my mail into a paper bag without looking at it.

On the morning that I returned to work, Cathy, the receptionist, stood up and came out from behind her desk, put her arms around my shoulders and pulled me to her. "I'm so sorry, Don," she said. As she held me, I had the sensation that my torso had become a rotted, hollow stump and that I might crack and fragment if Cathy squeezed just a bit harder but I didn't have the heart to pull away from her. I spent the morning going through the hundreds of e-mails that had piled up in my absence. "Raise Your Credit Rating," "Instant Equity Loan Approval," "H9427," "Staff Meeting Cancellation," "Christian Singles in Your Area," "Get a Degree in Law Enforcement," "Project Reports Due."

"Coffee, Don?" Palmer stood at the entrance to my cube. He wore his usual blue, Oxford cloth shirt and rumpled, pleated-front khaki pants. There was a small coffee stain at the bottom of his yellow and blue-patterned tie. I looked down at his left hand and noticed that the thin, white circle of skin on his ring finger was gone. It had been two months since he and Bettina split up. Now his life was in a lawyer's hands.

I glanced down at my hand and at my own wedding ring, a tarnished gold bridge between the two adjoining fingers. "Yeah, coffee," I said.

All the way down Court Street, I did my best to listen to Palmer, but the sound of his voice kept phasing in and out. It could have been the static-soaked sound of a radio signal from the other side of the world. "They're … the nights … blue … pause," Palmer was saying when a small, bright red and yellow plane zoomed across the street toward us and bounced over the curb.

It was not a plane. It was a bicycle, complete with three sets of wings and tail assembly. The man who piloted it wore a leather flying helmet and with round goggles that covered his eyes. "*Gott!*" he screamed as the bike pitched left, right then left at increasingly steeper angles. The bike's tires lost traction and the thing slid out from under him onto the sidewalk. "*Ach, scheisse!*" he yelled as he landed on his back, in front of us.

I walked over and squatted beside him. "Hurt?"

His eyes swam up at me behind the goggle lenses and blinked a few times. "I hate zees reconnaissance missions," he said.

"You're on a mission?"

He nodded over at the bike, which I realized was painted to look like a WWI German fighter plane, complete with two black crosses outlined in white on the top wing and the sides of the vertical stabilizer. "Zees Dr I's are tricky," he said, pulling off his goggles.

"Who were you looking for?" Palmer asked, as we helped him to his feet.

"The unusual. Things that stick out in the day," replied the man, bending over and righting the triplane, which was undamaged. He'd lost his German accent.

"Find anything?" I asked.

"Look around you," he yelled, as he mounted and pedaled down the sidewalk. He banked right and disappeared around the corner of Court and Church streets, leaving me staring after him, imagining him and his bike executing a climbing turn above the street, becoming a bright object diminishing against the blue sky.

"Good hunting, Baron," said Palmer.

Back at the office, I looked up the Dr I on the Internet. By the end of WWI, Fokker produced about three hundred of them for German flying corps. They were unstable death traps that ground looped on take off or came apart in the air, killing their pilots. The only person who seemed to like flying them was Manfred von Richthofen. Why would anyone take to the air in something like that? I asked myself, remembering the man's blue eyes and the gray wisps of hair curling out from beneath the edges of his helmet. Had I been with Ann, she would have queried him about the details of his flight. She might have asked the man to have coffee with us and to tell her about his plane's design and construction. Then she would have sent him off with a five-dollar bill for the squadron fund.

That night, I found the photograph I'd taken of Ann on our January,

Caribbean vacation. In the picture she stood waist deep in the blue-green water of the Tobago Cay beach. Behind Ann, the beach fringed by coconut palms curved away until it joined the line of the horizon. Above, a single, small cloud with a gray-smudged bottom hung in the pale blue expanse of sky. She'd begun to tire easily then, and her smile was strained as she squint-ed into the camera lens. Looking into the picture, I wondered if that cloud hanging behind my wife had been trying to tell me something, to warn me. I folded the picture and put it into my wallet.

I dreamed I was sitting behind the man on the bicycle, flying through the Caribbean sky. A few hundred of feet below us, the deep blue corduroy of the ocean rippled south and the air that swept past my head was warm and humid. The bike pilot put us through a gentle right turn above an is-land. From the shoreline, a woman stood beside a shopping cart waving up at us. She was too far away to see her face clearly. "Land this thing," I yelled at the back of the pilot's head. "*Nein!* Too little fuel," he screamed over the wind and pulled us up and away.

In the morning, my room smelled faintly of sea air. As I drove to work, I searched the downtown sidewalks for the woman with the shopping cart and the man on the triplane bike. They were not there. As I pulled into my parking spot, I noticed a woman sitting on the ground with her back against the concrete wall of the next office building. She was smoking a cigarette. Her head leaned back against the wall, eyes closed against the morning sun. The woman's blood hair seemed enmeshed with the wall of reflected, but-tery yellow light. I would have sworn the wall had given birth to her, ciga-rette and all. She was smiling softly. Perhaps she was listening to something, a voice or music, on the other side of the glowing wall, or maybe she was just enjoying the nicotine high of her first smoke of the morning.

In my cubicle, I concentrated on responding to e-mails and sorting through the remainder of stuff that had piled up in my in-box. But the woman beside the wall kept gently pushing her way into the right side of my head. On my desk, next to my computer monitor, a young Ann smiled up at me from a black-and-white photo I'd taken of her a few weeks after our wedding. When ten-o'clock came around I walked down the blue-car-peted hallway and took the stairs to sidewalk that led to the parking lot.

She was gone. Beside the spot where she'd sat, a cigarette butt lay on the asphalt smoked down to the filter. The angle of the sun had changed and the wall was now a flat, white expanse of concrete. I leaned forward, put my forehead to the wall and felt its coolness seep into my brow. Then I knelt down so that my face was inches from the spot on the wall where the woman had rested and I inhaled. Mixed with the scent of stale cigarette smoke was the smell of the woman's hair. I straightened and stepped back.

At that moment, I wanted the other wall, the one made of yellow light to return so that I could step through it and return to what I'd had. I told myself that this was grief, the residue of my dead wife. It was the fading scent of her in the fabric of the living room couch and the arrangement of the glasses and cups in the kitchen cupboard, the sight of her clothes hanging on her side of the bedroom closet, and her shoes lined up below the blouses, jackets, skirts and dresses that I didn't have the heart to remove. That was why I still slept on the left side of our queen-sized bed, beside the ghost of my wife. I turned and walked back into the building.

Back in my cubicle, when I logged on to the system, the screen did this flickering thing and then filled with the same impressionist light that had painted the wall that morning. I found myself unable to look away because the soft yellow had entered my head and its warmth worked its way down my neck and into my shoulders.

"Hey, Don. You okay?" asked Palmer from my cubicle entrance.

His face froze when I swiveled around in my chair. That's when I realized I'd been crying.

"It's the light," I said.

"What is it?"

"Can't you see it?"

"Don, maybe you should take the rest of the day off."

"Look," I replied turning halfway back to the monitor. My online mailbox stared back at me. The light was gone.

Palmer glanced at the screen and then at me. "Come on. Let's get out of here," he said.

"Yeah, sure," I said, feeling an edge of resentment at being pulled away from that warm emptiness.

We went out of the north entrance and walked east on Cartagena Street into a neighborhood of cheap apartment buildings and run-down, wood-framed houses. In the driveways and skinny parking lots, there were cars with dirty windshields and quarter panel dents. Tree roots shattered the sidewalk in places.

"You still going out with that woman who works at the bank?" I asked.

Geronimo G. Tagatac

"Angela? Not since last month."

"I had a dream about that guy on the bicycle."

"I wanted her to move in with me but she said that it was too soon."

"A woman I saw the morning after Ann died was in the dream, too."

"I'm tired of the post-divorce running around," Don said. "I want some stability in my life. But Angela wasn't ready to commit to one person."

"Palmer, have you ever felt like you're falling off the edge of things?"

"Do I ever. I was always the one who wanted more independence in my marriage and now I want to settle down. It's so crazy," he said, laughing softly.

"There was a woman sitting outside of the building this morning, Palmer. She didn't say anything, but I think she was trying to tell me something."

Palmer's mouth became a soft line and he looked down at the broken pavement. "You must have plenty of vacation time. Go somewhere else, get away from the house and the job."

"Where Palmer? Where do I go?"

"You need to take a vacation from yourself," he said

At noon, I walked downtown to La Casa de Bob's for lunch. I sat at an outdoor table shaded by a Corona Beer umbrella. This was where I'd sometimes meet Ann for lunch. The waitress, a stout woman in her forties, came over with two menus, napkin-wrapped silverware and a glass of water that she put down on the table. She handed me one of the menus and said, "I'll be back to take your order."

I sat and stared at the way the noontime shadows stained the sidewalk and I felt suddenly tired. And then a voice said, "It's hard to stay in the sun."

The old man stood ten feet away. Balding, he'd tied the white hair at the side of his head into a ponytail and bound the end of his beard so it made a sharp point against the middle of his chest. His green corduroy pants were clean but too short for his skinny legs. Over his shoulder, he carried a half-filled, duffel bag by one strap. He looked over at me with his blue eyes and smiled. "Slept at a construction site last night. No roof, just bare rafters and sky. I saw three shooting stars. The beginning and the end of the world at the same time."

"You need something?"

"No, no I'm fine. How about you, comrade?"

"I'm no longer sure of what I need," I replied.

"That's not a bad thing." He turned and walked away from me, up the sidewalk toward the flow of cross traffic, at High Street. His walk was the unhurried stride of those wandering, holy men you see in documentaries about India. All he needed was a walking staff.

After the old man had gone, I sat at my table and thought about the sea and the sky over the Caribbean and about the afternoons and evenings I'd spent with Ann on the afterdeck of the Yankee Clipper. I recalled the stern's rise and fall and the breeze against our faces and arms as we sailed northward. On the nights we slept on deck we lay, side-by-side, and watched the roving finger of the mizzenmast pointing out constellations in the expanse of stars and sky. I closed my eyes and inhaled, trying hard to recall the smell of Ann's hair mixed with that of the ocean and found that it was faint but still with me, though it was mingled in with the smell of my enchilada and refries.

If I sat at that table long enough maybe the shopping cart woman and the man on the flying bicycle would return. Perhaps the woman in the wall of light would appear. I wondered if I'd ever see the wandering old man again who wanted to reassure me that things would work out. I pulled the beach photo I'd taken of Ann out of my wallet and unfolded it. There, against the cloud behind her head, was a tiny speck. Perhaps it was a flaw in the photo. It could have been a distant airliner, or even a red and yellow bicycle with three sets of wings.

The Calling
by Eileen Pettycrew

1.
Sounds from Swan Island swim up:
clangs, clatters, bells,
hammering, metal on metal.
Voices behind me drift
toward the bluff. The wind
that carries them blows naked
across the grass, leaving
no footprint, no public
display of affection,
only a quick and discreet
caress, just enough to lift
the hair on my arm. Then it's gone—
to move clouds, fill a sail.

2.
A writer edges to the edge:
Curtains open, expose
dark circles.

California Aqueduct looms
before her; she jumps. Slant
concrete keeps

her in as she floats, as water
becomes her ink; she waits
to become

irrigation, flowing to root,
stem, leaf, to the one grape
one of you

recognizes as your own.

3.
Oh fog,
oh inner space,
what compels us
to shape bone
into words, grind up
a mix of ash and bruise,
line it up on a page?

All those blue dragonflies at the reservoir,
the hours you spent trying to catch one,
and one day you did, and it was electrifying,
that wild blue inside your jar.

The Honeymoon House
by Tim Schell

It had been a hunting incident, is what Jack Crabtree told the sheriff, an incident, he said, pronouncing each of the three syllables individually, and as he mouthed the sounds he thought he should have replaced the "in" with "acc," but it was too late for that, and the sheriff just looked at him long and hard. Jack and his father had been hunting pheasant across the creek by the Honeymoon House, a ramshackle homestead cabin leaning under the weight of all the years since the westward migration, a clapboard cabin built in the sheltered valley by some erstwhile family settling in the Oregon Territory 150 years before, arriving in a rickety wagon, maybe, with a few buckets of seeds and maybe a cow and some chickens and a young girl in a blue bonnet sitting on the bench seat between her mother and father. This is how Jack always imagined it, the vision arising each fall when he and his father would cross the creek and walk up to the house where there were often quail feeding. Some thirty years had passed since Jack had first hunted here as a boy, and nothing had changed except the house may have slumped a little more under the weight of each of those years. The brown hills were still the same. The clear creek still gurgled. The morning autumn air still a crisped chill.

The house stood with dilapidated portals sighing in the wind that blew down out of the rocky canyons that rose above the valley floor set on the south sector of this wheat farm and cattle ranch owned by his father's old high school friend Dick McGregor, a wiry man with a wry sense of humor who told each of his five daughters about the house he was proud to give them as a place to spend a quiet honeymoon. The place came to be known throughout Morrow County as the Honeymoon House, and those who hunted here sometimes holed up in the shelter if a rare but welcomed rain came through the valley.

"An incident?" the sheriff asked. "What do you mean by incident?" He held a notepad in his left hand and a pencil in his right. His lower lip bulged with chaw, and he spat from time to time.

Jack leaned against the hood of his Ford pickup parked next to Mc-

Gregor's barn. Two guns lay on the hood, a twelve gauge pump and the double-barrel sixteen gauge his father had made in Ibar, Spain, when Jack was sixteen and he and his family traveled through Europe. Now it was thirty years later, and his father lay dead in the bed of the truck. Jack stroked the stock of the Spanish gun.

"We were crossing through the fence, and dad had set the gun down. I set mine down, too. When I pulled up the strand of barbwire, his gun slipped. It went off when it hit the ground, I guess."

The morning sun shined so Jack had to squint. He held his hand up to shade his eyes. "I don't know what to say," he said.

The sheriff wiped his chin with an open palm. He turned his head, spat, and wiped his mouth with the back of his hand that held the notepad. "I understand. But how is it the gun shot up into the air to hit him in the chest when the gun was falling down? That's what I don't understand."

Jack reached into the breast pocket of the red Filson jacket he wore, and pulled out a pack of Marlboros. He had quit three years before, but had recently started again. He had quit and started so many times that he joked he was trying to get hooked, but it just never quite took. "Dad was lacing up his boots when the gun went off. I guess that explains it."

The sheriff sighed. He walked back around to the tailgate. Jack watched him as he looked down at the body of his father. He spat on the ground and wiped his mouth again before coming back to the front of the truck where Jack stood smoking. "It was not an incident," the sheriff said, spitting again. "It was an accident. It's an entirely different word."

When Jack was fifteen, he came home from school one fall day after football practice, and his dad was already home from work, the red Corvair parked beneath the basketball hoop in the driveway. Jack went in through the garage door.

Upstairs, he found his dad sitting on the sofa with his bad leg resting on the ottoman—an empire all its own, his dad joked—a can of Blitz beer on the end table by his side. His father had been in a car accident the previous fall, and he still wore the steel brace that went from the sole of his foot all the way up to his hip. It had happened just after he had left for work, and Jack and his mom were finishing up breakfast before school. When they heard the siren, his mother said, "God, that's David. Something's happened to David."

A minute later—or so it seemed now, though Jack couldn't be sure—Mrs. Murphy was at the door telling Jack's mom about the accident, about the ambulance, about which hospital it was off to, and Jack's mom told him to get to school, that she would let him know later what they were to do.

It must have been shock, Jack now thought, that had confused his mother into telling him to get to school when he did not know what had happened to his father, that led him to the bus stop where he saw his dad's crumpled blue 1968 BMW in the ditch, shattered glass frosting the road. He did as he was told: he went to school, and after school Mrs. Murphy picked him up and drove him to football practice as his father had directed from his hospital bed in the ICU, and it wasn't until after practice that he was allowed to go to the hospital to see his father who lay in traction.

That was a year earlier. Now Jack was home from school.

"How's the leg?" He sat down on the sofa across from his father.

"Good. Getting better every day."

"Good."

"How was school?"

"Fine. I got an A on the French test."

"*Félicitations.*" He picked up the beer can, took a sip, and sighed. "Grandpa called five times today."

"Did he ask for the boss?"

"That's what your mother said. He told her he wants to go home."

"He's getting more confused every day, isn't he, Dad?"

"Seems like it. Mom said he called fifteen times yesterday."

"Dad, will you ..."

"Will I what?"

"Ever be like grandpa?"

"Old? I hope so."

"No. You know what I mean."

"No. I never want to be like that."

"Yeah, me neither."

"Not ever. Do you know what I mean? Never."

Jack asked his father if he could have a sip of beer, and his father handed him the can. It was a nightly ritual, one Jack often recollected when he would drink beer out of a can. It was hoppy, and the bubbles backed up his nose. He didn't like the taste so much as he liked the fact that he and his father shared a can of beer.

"Grandpa's getting pretty confused. What are we going to do?"

"I don't know yet. I just don't know."

On the Sunday before, Jack had driven to the assisted-living facility and picked up his grandfather as he did almost every Sunday when he would bring him home for dinner.

When Jack got to his grandfather's room, he found him watching television in his pajamas. "Gramps," he said. "Let's get you dressed so we can go have dinner."

"Dinner? I haven't had breakfast. Where are we going?"

"To our house. It's Sunday. We'll go have Sunday dinner."

"We're going home?"

"Yep," Jack said as he helped his grandfather stand, gently tugging his arms.

"Mom's made roast beef and mashed potatoes and your favorite: Lemon meringue pie."

The golden sunlight shined through the trees, the leaves of which had changed color but had not yet fallen. Jack drove through Washington Park past children playing in the water fountain and people slinging Frisbees. People sat on out-stretched blankets eating picnic dinners for maybe the last time before the evenings became too chilly to sit outside. The oak, maple, and alder tree leaves colored orange against the green of the Douglas firs.

They drove up the winding road with the windows down.

"I like the smell," his grandfather said.

"Me too."

"It smells fresh."

"It does."

"Are you married yet?"

Jack smiled. He reached across and patted his grandfather on the shoulder. "No, Gramps. Not yet. I'm only sixteen."

"Oh, I thought you might be. Some good looker with long legs."

"No, not yet."

"You tell me when you are."

"I'll do that. For sure."

Jack's mother served dinner, roast beef with rich brown gravy, steaming mashed potatoes and sautéed green beans. After dinner they had pie and coffee with Jack sitting across from his grandfather and his father and mother sitting at each end of the dining room table. His mother poured more coffee, and his grandfather took a sip before reaching into the inside breast pocket of his sports jacket and taking out a pack of Camels and a book of matches. Everyone watched him as he put a cigarette between his lips, struck a match and lit it before exhaling a stream of smoke, and setting the match in the saucer that held his coffee cup.

"Dad?" Jack's father said.

"What?" Inhaling again. "You want one? Sally? You Jack?"

"What are you doing?" Jack's father asked.

"What does it look like I'm doing? I'm having a cigarette."

"I see that. But you don't smoke."

"I don't?" Now the old man looked confused and depressed at this news that he didn't smoke. Yet he was smoking. He stared at the lit cigarette in his right hand. He rolled it between his thumb and forefinger, back and forth, looking at it as if he were mulling over some great decision to be made.

Everyone was quiet.

"No, Dad. You quit twenty years ago."

"I did?" He looked saddened but resigned to this new surprise life had pulled on him. He snuffed out the cigarette in his coffee and set the butt next to the match. He picked up the coffee cup and sipped before setting the cup back down. No one said another word about the incident.

Jack's father took the last sip from the can of Blitz. "How about a game of cribbage before dinner?"

"Sure thing. I'll beat you this time."

"What happened the last time we played?"

"Funny. I don't remember." Jack's father had skunked him.

They played the game as Jack's mother cooked dinner. They could smell the corned beef and cabbage as the evening light fell to dusk and then the street lamps came on. Jack turned the cards of the crib over and saw that he had nothing in his hand, so he said, "What the little boy shot at."

His father smiled, maybe in the memory of how those words had been passed down from his own father, six simple words signifying *nothing, nada, rien de tout*, his own father saying it on cold winter evenings in their little house on the North Dakota prairie so many years before.

When dinner came this fall night, Jack's father and mother told him that they were going to Europe, that life was too short and too tenuous not to do something a bit unreserved, that Jack's dad was quitting his job and they were selling the house: they were going to drive around Europe for a year.

Jack said, "What about school?" He could not imagine not going to school.

They said he could go to school in England and in France and that would be plenty because he could read books as they traveled, and that is what they did, and when they arrived in Ibar, Spain, they went to the factory that Jack's dad had read about, the famous place where they made shotguns by hand, and that winter morning they found themselves in a large office with mahogany walls and a teak desk wide enough to sleep on with a window behind the desk opening up onto the town that rolled out beneath them.

The company president spoke good English, but with a heavy accent, and a woman brought in a silver tray with coffee cups and both his father and the man with slicked back black hair smoked cigars and looked at pictures of fancy shotguns with wispy waves of silver inlay.

Upon the consummation of the deal, the two men shook hands, and they were shown out of the office and escorted to their car with great fanfare, Jack thought, so much fanfare over the purchase of a shotgun.

Jack had been sixteen.

Now Jack was forty-five, and he drove the truck down the gravel road, smoking a cigarette and drinking coffee from his thermos. As he crossed the cattle-guard onto the paved two-lane, he remembered his grandfather, and then his thoughts turned to his father who lay in the bed of the truck. Jack's wife and son were back in Portland waiting for him to return, and he hadn't yet called them to tell them about his father, but he would have to tell them soon enough.

As he drove through the Columbia River Gorge, the wind whipping white caps off the river surface beneath somber palisades, the sun disappeared behind the mountains and the light went purple and then dark. The stars were out and it was cold with the coming winter. As he drove, Jack thought about his father earlier that day as they drove into the ranch and how his eyes lit up at seeing the grain elevators.

They had driven along the dirt track until they came to the creek, and across the sinewy thread of water they could see the Honeymoon House. Jack's dad had smiled and said, "You know, Jack, all of Dick's daughters had their honeymoons there. Saved Dick a lot of money."

Jack hadn't said anything in answer and they climbed out of the truck,

Jack carrying the sixteen gauge, the twelve gauge left behind. They walked across a wide plank spanning the water. When they came to the barbed wire fence, Jack helped his father through to the other side, the double-barreled sixteen gauge from Ibar, Spain, breaking the morning's silence, an incident before the Honeymoon House on a Sunday morning in late autumn with the sun caught behind a cloud.

Ballet in the Park
by Ada Molinoff

A back straightens, an arm begins
to lift. I see which members of the audience
were dancers. Movement rediscovers
dormant pathways, triggers

imperceptible leaps: when a ballerina
tour-jetés my leg muscles twitch.
We watch closely—
our bodies remember.

Wanting What Somebody Else Has

by Penelope Schott

With whole body devotion, my dog
gnaws her neglected rawhide bone

after a visiting dog has chewed it
to mush. The spit of another dog

has rendered it precious. Listen
to the skritch of her molars –

such gratified concentration,
her tail out flat behind her.

And what is it I covet? The girl
who checked out my groceries

couldn't see that she was lovely.
Because I can't steal her beauty,

I just stole two ripe strawberries
from the neighbors' rock wall –

so sweet. Who still remembers
the nipples of my young breasts?

Today I covet the long-lived world.
Little yellow strawberry seeds

prickle the
tongue.

Dorothy Is Surprised
by Judith Arcana

When she turned 75 in 2010, Dorothy suddenly found casual masturbation once again interested her. She was surprised. Soon after her 60th birthday she'd stopped fucking entirely and forgot (mostly) about masturbation. Oh, some occasional nostalgic affectionate strokes, sure, but nothing much. At 75 though (for which she'd had a party with balloons and cupcakes and friends from the library), her clitoris, quite suddenly, reasserted itself.

What a surprise! Sex had become a memory, a source of occasional recollection. At first she simply played herself to sleep, the lips of her vulva like a thickly stringed instrument. She resumed the stroking she'd always loved, loving the softly damp red folds she'd see in the little round mirror between her thighs, opening herself slowly, flashlighting the vaginal cave in search of its mythic heart, the cervix rose.

She thought, Well! She wondered, Do I have time for this? I suppose it'll be fine if I rock myself to sleep and wake myself up sticky—it's not a social event; no planning necessary, I don't have to look good, I needn't *dress* for it. She laughed.

Then one day she stood next to a young woman in line at the farmers market—they were waiting to pay for their radishes, brilliant springtime red, smoothly red like 40s lipstick. They talked and laughed and walked over to the tamale stand—they both ordered the one with artichokes and cheese and chose the spicy salsa. When Dorothy put her radishes in the young woman's refrigerator, she thought, Am I actually *doing* this? With this child? (Her name was Kimberly, one of the fifteen most popular girl's names in 1980, the year Dorothy turned 45.) Am I actually doing this?

A couple weeks later, when she brought the young man from the anti-GMO rally home with her, she had some bad thoughts while he locked up his bike. Not self-doubt, not derision. Contrition maybe? Maybe that old fashioned kind of embarrassed question again: What *am* I doing with these children? The emotional spasm passed, making way for orgasmic spasms she was now experiencing as an anthropologist, a trekker over her own terrain, entering the valley and walking barefoot through the freshets that rush to fill the river's main channel. The young man was named Ryan, and Dorothy thought he might do well with Kimberly. Both of them traced the wrinkles of her face as lightly as they licked the folds of her labia and the pebbled nipples of her long silken breasts.

She couldn't—wouldn't want to—do this often. She wondered if it *meant* something, if it was somehow *important*, this resurgence of desire, this re-emergence of vulvar demand. Did it have symbolic value? She'd been healthy for years, since she began to take herself seriously, since her back injury taught her how to live differently in her body, since maintenance became conscious and daily. This, she decided, was like the birthday cupcakes, like their frosting—adorable, sweet and creamy, quick little bits, treats. Not central like friendship, not like walking, talking, thinking and reading. Not crucial, like trees and rivers. Maybe not even organic, so out of the ordinary and *extra* as it was. And, given the ongoing turning of the earth and her own body, probably not sustainable. These were little treats—their importance and value derived from their sudden surprising appearance, like wild flowers beside the trail, like the scarlet flash of a redwinged blackbird.

She thought: These young ones, this flash of my body—this must be to show me, again, there's always something new, there's never anything new; everything is the same while it's different; I keep changing even though I'll always be who I am—and being wise doesn't mean there's no surprise.

Spring Visions
by Nazifa Islam

There's so much we can't be witness to.
Imagination leaves us wanting
and now there's spring being shipped off:

a red train station – the conductor sending
on car after car of tulips and bubbling
mud from forests in northern Atlantis.

Flowers and warmth – that's all we want.
We sit and wait for our own car
it might not be coming

Walk to the Gym
by Jean Rover

I hurried out the backdoor on a brisk, dark morning to use the gym at the school. It was eerie being on the street alone so early and a little risky—especially since an elderly woman was murdered in our neighborhood. It was right after Labor Day, when people start thinking about picking apples, turning the soil in their gardens one last time, and storing their white shoes. Someone broke into her house and stabbed her. They never did finger the guy who did it.

The nippy wind cut through my sweats. I wrapped my faded Indian blanket snuggly around my shoulders; the one I got a while back with green stamps. Why did I leave the warmth of my bed to do this? I needed to exercise that was why, and once I did, I would feel warm again. And calmer. My doctor said exercise would be good for me. I know he said that because I wrote it down.

A street light splashed a yellow glow across the wet pavement. Some of the houses already had big orange pumpkins displayed on porches smiling their crooked grins. A ghost made from a white sheet flapped high in a tree. I felt the slick leaves that covered the sidewalk squish under my feet. I slowed my pace to avoid slipping.

An ashy smell hung in the air. That, I knew, came from the smoke that constantly belched from the Beeler's chimney. Ray Beeler always brought a big stack of wood in the fall. "There's nothin' that warms a house like wood heat," he'd brag. As soon as the temperature dipped, he'd get up early and packed a hefty bundle of it over wadded newspaper into that old woodstove they had in the family room. Then, by golly, he'd take a match to it. My Al said, "One of these days, he was gonna burn the house down."

I turned my attention back to the leafy street. That was when I saw him.

The shadowy figure of a large man came toward me. He wore a dark overcoat and a black cap. A red, wool scarf peeked from his collar. No one else was around and no cars passed. I crossed to the other side. The man kept coming, continually looking in my direction. I let the blanket slip from my shoulders, so I'd be free to run. I cut down an alley and through an empty lot. I heard him running too, making heavy breathing sounds like a horse after a race. I didn't stop until I reached the corner and saw the schoolyard lights.

Out of breath, I pulled open the heavy door to the gym and made my way inside. I blended in with the children and began walking slowly around the perimeter until my breathing became normal. Actually, I was surprised to see so many kids there at such an early hour. They were running, jumping, yelling, and tossing balls. I ducked to avoid a wayward basketball that almost hit me in the head, but I kept walking until I heard a whistle.

The sound came from a portly man in a black-and-white striped shirt. He blew on his whistle again and started a class. There were so many kids; it was impossible to continue on my own. I found myself in the midst of them trying to do the things the instructor man demanded. For some reason, he constantly corrected me. "Sit up straight. Shoulders back and down," he barked. I got exhausted doing the sit-ups, so I just laid down right there on the floor. I didn't care what he said. He stood over me, shook his head, and smirked. Why was I getting all this attention? Surely, he knew I wasn't a student. As far as I could tell, I was the only other adult there. Still, I tried the best I could to do the exercises correctly, but I was getting a little annoyed.

Once the bell rang, everyone scampered off. I was alone in the gym and glad of it. I decided I would not go back there again. It was never like this before. No, I'd ask the doctor to write me an excuse. I wasn't going to do jumping jacks again. Ever.

It was still dark and cold outside when I started back toward my house. I searched the street for my blanket, but found only a tattered, yellow corduroy potholder that someone had tossed. In a strange way, it was comforting. It looked like the kind my mother made out of scrap material from the big bag she stored in the back of her closet. Those were the days. I missed Al, too. I needed him now more than ever.

I saw a woman tending potted plants on the porch of her rundown house. She had apparently found my blanket and used it to protect them from the frost. I stood for a moment, clutching my potholder. She flicked on the porch light, reached for a broom and began sweeping her front steps. With that hooked nose of hers, she looked like a real live witch. I stared at the blanket and up at her. She didn't speak but gave me an ugly, suspicious scowl, so it didn't feel right for me to grab my blanket. After all, I had thrown it down on the street. Finders keepers, they used to say.

I hurried away when that sudden eerie feeling came back. It was hard to describe. The area seemed familiar enough, but strange, too. I could not find my house. I sniffed the air for smoke, but couldn't locate the Beeler place either. If I could just smell the smoke, I'd know I was close. I must have taken the wrong street. But how could that be when my blanket was back there? Maybe I walked too far. How could I be lost in my own neighborhood? Al and I used to walk here all the time when the kids were little. Maybe someone moved the street sign. Maybe it was a Halloween prank. Well, it wasn't funny.

Then he was again! *That man.* I knew it was he because of his red scarf. He stared at me. Oh my God, he was coming closer. I knew he was after me.

I was almost to the corner, so I turned and ran. Several dogs barked in the distance. That was good. Maybe someone would look out a window. I crouched down behind a big rhododendron bush on the side of a white house and waited. I heard his footsteps against the sidewalk. His shoes squeaked as he came closer. Through the bush, I saw his dark pant legs. I watched them as they went by. Then he turned, and I watched them go by again.

Soon, it would get lighter. Maybe I should hide here until then. I wished now that I'd never left my house. The cold gave me goose bumps, and I missed my cozy kitchen. When I got home, I was going to make a big pot of coffee and sit in front of the fire. Coffee fixed everything. My knees ached from squatting, and the branches poked my chest. If Al were here, we'd snuggle and I'd get warm. I wouldn't have to crouch behind any dang bush either.

I checked my pocket, but couldn't feel my keys. There was nothing in there but a cough drop. A wave of panic surged through my stomach. In my haste, I must have left the keys on the counter or maybe I lost them at the gym or on the street. Oh God. How would I get in now? What if I forgot to lock the door? What if someone was in my house? What if it was that man! I leaped from the protection of the bush and ran back to the corner and down the street.

Then I stopped.

The man stepped out from behind a tree. He was right in front of me. My hands shook as I backed away. He carried a big black bag. What was in there? A gun? Rope? Or maybe a knife?

"Who are you?" I asked, trying to sound brave. "What do you want?"

"Edith." He smiled and reached his hand toward me.

Edith? "Murderer!" I yelled. "I know who you are. You're that mur-
derer!"

"Edith," he said again.

"You stay away from me! I'll scream if you come closer."

He reached into his bag.

"Stop right there." I doubled my fists to look menacing and bounced on
my feet like a boxer ready to land a punch.

"Edith, please. Look, I brought Al."

He pulled a big, white stuffed rabbit out of the bag and thrust it to
toward me. It's ears flopped over and one eye was missing.

"I'm here to help," he said. "You wandered away from the hospital
again."

I hugged Al close and stroked his soft head. I could even smell smoke
from the Beeler's chimney.

Listings
by Amy Miller

How ill they fit,
the houses on the row.
How like a rack of scratchy suits
they hang from chimneys.

How their eyes blink hollow
in windows stripped of shades,
bare ribs of wood floor
shivering in empty air.

How each owner knew them,
jogged a door with a knee
or painted the windows shut
in the first warm week of marriage.

How they hunch and sigh,
their shingles pressing in,
their lilacs bravely budding
beside the empty driveway.

At the End of a Season
by Marilyn Johnston

There's a bucket
of radishes
left by the gate.
A two-bushel sack
of golden potatoes
set down beside
the back door.
Half-green tomatoes
still on the vine,
brought in to ripen
in the old shed—
shielded
from the first frost.

A hoe and an old
rusty shovel
leaned up against
the barn wall,
and two worn
lawn chairs
he always said
he'd reweave
one day,
tucked into
one another.

His old straw hat
on a hook, waiting.

Dam It
by Kelly Kittel

You have probably never heard of Lonesome Larry, but he was a pretty famous fish in his day. In 1992, Larry was the only sockeye salmon to successfully make the journey of over nine hundred miles from the Pacific Ocean to Redfish Lake. His ancestors swam this course for thousands of years, but for the past fifty or so, Larry and his fellow fish had the additional challenge of navigating past eight dams. As spring turned to summer, Larry began his homeward journey as a silver fish with a blue back in the prime of his life. He swam a few hundred miles along the riparian border of Oregon and Washington as the river water changed from brackish to fresh, then took the Snake River into Idaho where he climbed almost seven thousand feet to the sweet waters of his natal lake, nestled high in the Sawtooth Mountains.

Like all sockeye, as Larry neared his spawning habitat, his body color changed to ruby red and his head and tail turned green. Being a male, he also developed a humped back and a hooked snout filled with sharp canine teeth. His transformation complete, he'd become both a fierce opponent to the other males and oh-so-desirable to blushing females. Historically, Redfish Lake had filled each fall with some thirty thousand sockeye, transforming its waters into the passionate color of the spawning fish. But the intended reward for Larry's perseverance on his month-long feat of endurance was conspicuously absent when he arrived.

I imagine Larry's excitement at reaching his destination must have quickly turned to disappointment as he swam around and around the lake in vain. No attractive female fish wagged her tail provocatively at Larry. No sexy salmonid arrived soon after with whom he could co-mingle his genetic material on the gravelly bottom of their pristine alpine lake. Larry found himself all alone in the lake formerly known for its abundance of red fish. Well, not quite alone, but not with the lovely lady he'd hoped to dance with. Instead, some not-so-sexy scientists waited for him in the cold, clear water, excited in their own way to see Larry. They captured him, milked his sperm, then froze and stored it.

><((((°>.....><((((°>.....><((((°>.....><((((°>.....><((((°>...

While Larry was still a wee smolt, I began working as a fish biologist for the Bonneville Power Administration (BPA). BPA kept the toasters toasting from Tidewater to Twisp and the blenders blending from Bingen to Boring in the Pacific Northwest. BPA was a federal power-marketing agency, meaning they sold the electricity generated by the federally owned dams on the Columbia. The river flowed in hundreds of millions of gallons per minute, producing a staggering amount of hydropower and the lowest electrical rates in our nation. There was only one effective way to capture the benefits of these free-flowing river water molecules: build a dam.

By the time I moved to Oregon in 1991, there were over 274 dams of all shapes and sizes in the Columbia River basin, dams that had already changed the entire ecosystem of the main stem as well as her hundreds of tributaries. The Columbia was a colossal river, impressive for its sheer magnitude: 1,243 miles long; it formed most of the border between Washington and Oregon for three hundred miles, before turning north and winding up through the Evergreen State into the grizzly wilderness of Canada.

I wish I'd known the Columbia before all those dams tamed her from a river of reckoning into a series of slackwater lakes. I arrived too late to see her fly, big and wild, annually flooding everything downstream with her voluminous spring runoff. In her glory days, she'd flushed baby salmon to sea, tail-first, hidden safely in the murky grains of dirt from across her vast watershed. In my day, fourteen dams impeded her infamous flow, forcing the smolts to work their tails off as they swam head-first to the Pacific. And when they encountered each concrete stop sign on their journey, powerful currents pinned their tiny bodies against the cold, hard surface or swept them through the spinning turbines.

BPA had spent billions of dollars trying to deliver smolts safely around the dams and mitigate the myriad of impacts on fish and wildlife. And people. Each year the Northwest Power Planning Council designed the menu of projects BPA would fund from their gourmet budget. They tossed every conceivable proposal into a big pot and everyone hovered around, spoons in hand, waiting to be fed. Much of what my fellow Mayflower descendants called "wampum" went to Native American tribes for projects like platinum-plated experimental fish hatcheries, the subject of great controversy. My job was to help save the salmon by managing a platter of these projects, including the Snake River Sockeye Captive Broodstock Program to rescue the offspring of Lonesome Larry and a smorgasbord of projects for the Yakima Indian Nation.

I enjoyed the historical romance I felt as a twelfth generation descendant of the Pilgrims working with Native Americans. I felt we had an obligation to the original inhabitants of our country and was ashamed that my ancestors had broken every treaty ever signed with them. Our forefathers gave finger-crossed promises to the tribes, granting them the rights to hunt and to fish for as long as the rivers ran—essential rights they used to inherit at birth, like breathing. To their credit, BPA tried to make reparations for the hollow echoes of those words, but salmon populations were still on an overall decline and the theories as to why were more abundant than the fish themselves. Dubbed the four H's, the impacts mostly fell under the categories of hydropower, hatcheries, habitat, and harvest. One thing was certain, the one big H was humans and we'd spent a lot of wampum figuring out just how little we understood.

><((((°>.....><((((°>.....><((((°>.....><((((°>.....><((((°>...

Larry was lucky. Other legendary salmon had no projects devoted to their survival, existing today only in story, song, and memory. Once upon a time, there lived a species of summer Chinook called June Hogs, which swam the entire length of the Columbia, following their noses on a marathon journey of over one thousand miles to the familiar scent of their natal stream in Canada. These fish averaged around seventy pounds but often grew to be over one hundred. When Mother Nature called her salmon home to their natal streams to spawn, they stopped eating. This was their final hurrah, their race to ensure their genetic survival but their individual death. "Spawn and Die" was their battle cry in the final frenzied days of their lives. They swam until their skin shredded off, until they arrived, transformed, at the place smelling of their birth. The June Hogs had to be huge in order to endure their long journey without eating, or they would never have made it. Like Larry's ancestors, they didn't have any dams to negotiate.

When it comes to dams, Grand Coulee was undoubtedly the Granddaddy of them all. It was one of the world's largest dams and the single largest producer of electricity in our nation, generating hundreds of millions of dollars annually. Coulee was also a giant watering can, irrigating half a million acres and transforming river water into apples, pears, and cherries ripening in vast orchards where once was dry desert. Coulee was one mile wide and the largest concrete slab in the world, three to four times the size of the Great Pyramid. The spillway was twice the height of Niagara Falls and its reservoir, Lake Roosevelt, extended one hundred and fifty miles to the Canadian border. As Coulee neared completion in 1941, BPA hired Woody Guthrie to compose songs about the Columbia River with the intent of rallying public support for the building of Coulee and other dams. Woody was so inspired by the majestic beauty of the Columbia Basin, he wrote twenty-six songs about it in one month.

Salmon spend the bulk of their lives swimming around the cold Pacific Ocean with whales and playing hide and seek in kelp beds. So for three to five years after Coulee was completed, the legendary June Hogs came happily swimming some six hundred miles upstream, only to find this mysterious marvel of modern engineering blocking the survival of their species. The Great Grand Coulee Dam eliminated their access to the remaining six hundred miles of the Columbia, itself, as well as over eleven hundred miles of their upstream spawning habitat. As Woody sang his siren songs, these magnificent fish heaved themselves again and again at the concrete slab, attempting to jump five hundred feet over it but ultimately beating themselves to death. Woody wasn't hired, after all, to write songs about them. Following the trail left by the seventy-seven men who'd died constructing Coulee, the bodies of the June Hogs were lovingly buoyed away by the river waters in which they were born, floating downstream in the swirling current and spinning slowly in its eddies. The oceanic elements in their decomposing flesh nourished the river and fed the generations of salmon yet to come.

Now, the Bureau of Reclamation proudly entertains us with dancing electric salmon shows, lighting up the Coulee spillway nightly and casting shadows on Chinook cherries growing in nearby orchards. But that dam eliminated a race of fish and ended their stories.

><((((°>.....><((((°>.....><((((°>.....><((((°>.....><((((°>...

I am part fish and have spent most of my life swimming in one place or another, including across the Columbia River. Last Labor Day, I arose before sunrise along with some five hundred other swimmers and boarded the sternwheeler *Columbia Gorge* in Hood River, Oregon. We guzzled cups of coffee with the strawberry-pink snow cone of Mt. Hood reflected in our wake as the giant wheel pulled us across calm water. As the river rolled by, Judy—my swimming friend—was inspired to sing one of Woody's most famous BPA ballads, "Roll on, Columbia," and soon we had a rollicking choir. Judy was a librarian, a keeper of information, so I wasn't too surprised to discover she knew every verse of what was now the official Washington folk song. For me, constrained to crooning mostly the chorus, it was impressive to hear the multitude of others who kept apace with Judy, working their way through verse after obscure verse. A transplant from New England, I marveled at these folks who were, like my own husband, so firmly rooted in their Pacific Northwest heritage. We'd all flown or driven from far and wide to get to this moment. Sleep deprived and nearly naked, we joined our voices in song, preparing for our baptism in the waters now flowing from our lips.

As the last chorus faded to anticipation, the giant paddle wheel stopped turning and the boat came about on the shores of White Salmon, Washington. Then one by one, in wave after wave, we climbed out onto the ship's bow rail, plugged our noses, and leapt into the river. We adjusted our goggles and took the first of hundreds of strokes back across the Columbia towards the pointy peak of Mt. Hood. Silky water slipped through our fingers and filled our mouths with cool sweetness while Woody's words played in an endless wrap around our neon orange-capped heads.

Since it was Labor Day, I thought about the thousands of gaunt workers of Roosevelt's Works Progress Administration, the WPA, who'd come from far and wide to toil in obscurity, adding their sweat and tears to the water in my mouth. These brave and desperate men were mostly remembered for the things they'd left behind; they never became famous like Woody—the singer who gave them all a voice.

In between each of my strokes, I turned my face towards the basaltic bottom, scanning the green waters for the shadows of June Hogs. After each breath, I paused, listening underwater for the echoes of Celilo Falls. Remembering.

><((((°>.....><((((°>.....><((((°>.....><((((°>.....><((((°>...

The dam building had continued. In spite of our promises to the tribes who'd lived and fished along the river for thousands of years, Bonneville

Dam parted the waters in 1938, eliminating thirty-five native fishing sites and permanently blocking the migration of white sturgeon to their upstream spawning areas. It also enabled us to swim across the smooth river upstream. Two decades later, the Dalles Dam was completed, allowing us to swim across the river downstream. Like so many things, they named the reservoir behind the Dalles Dam for what it had destroyed—Celilo—the oldest inhabited village in America. Lewis and Clark had visited Celilo in 1805, calling it a "great emporium ... where all the neighboring nations assemble" with a population density unlike anything they'd seen on their long journey.

Likened to "The Wall Street of the West," the sound of Celilo had not been the ringing of a bell, but the roar of Celilo Falls. This sacred native fishing spot featured some five hundred wooden platforms suspended out over the falls like toothpick projects. Native men balanced precariously, scooping their long-handled dip nets into the raging waters below as muscular salmon leapt from pool to pool, traversing their way up the falls. For over fifteen thousand years, both the salmon and the people who'd worshipped them had proven themselves with feats of great agility and perseverance.

When the Dalles Dam was completed in 1957, tribal elders gathered on the dawn of a new shore. They gazed, unblinking, from the wrinkled folds of their wise faces like doulas at the birth of the quiet lake before them. As they searched their hearts and minds for what had been, Lake Celilo rose behind the dam, submerging the fishing platforms and drowning the village of Celilo. The roaring falls, beating with the rhythm of their very own hearts, were slowly silenced along with their voices as the sounds of Celilo became only a memory in a mere six hours.

><((((°>.....><((((°>.....><((((°>.....><((((°>.....><((((°>...

Larry's sperm lived on to become the basis for a successful captive breeding program for his progeny, still the most endangered salmon stock in the evergreen Pacific Northwest. Even though Larry will never meet the woman of his dreams, his milt is used to artificially fertilize the eggs of any female who swims to Redfish Lake, thereby eliminating that nasty little variable—timing. Today, Larry's offspring begin their lives in the cool air of a lab, not the lake, but they're ultimately set free in her fir-lined waters with the prayer they will successfully negotiate past the dams to the sea and come whistling back again some day.

As for Larry? They stuffed the poor guy, mounted him, and hung him on the Governor's wall. Not a very auspicious ending for such a celebrated fish, although I'm sure he draws an admiring glance every now and again from members of a species he never intended to attract. Larry's preservation was permanent; his fellow fish may not be so lucky. Slowly, Redfish Lake is beginning to shine again with flashes of crimson each fall. We can only hope that, like Larry, it will one day shimmer more red than green again.

God Becomes a Hairdresser

by Penelope Schott

Things are going badly. Handbasket badly.

What sort of things? you ask.

The usual: wars, the Red Sox season, those wild cells proliferating
to kill.

So God borrows scissors from the Three Fates and opens a salon
downtown, unisex, no less.

People come and sit in the chairs under nylon bibs like agreeable
oversized babies while God runs His holy fingers through their hair.

He clips and snips and sprays them with lotions. He twiddles and
crunches and poufs, and holds up a mirror behind, until His clients
look and see that it is good.

At 8 p.m, God combs out a last perm, accepts a tip, and pulls down
the shades.

So has His work made this world any better? Beats me.

Gold-Trimmed Prophet, What's the Use?

by Chelsea R. G. Kachman

Also the word of the Lord came unto me, saying, Son of man, behold, I take away from thee the desire of thine eyes with a stroke: yet neither shalt thou mourn nor weep, neither shall thy tears run down. Forbear to cry, make no mourning for the dead, bind the tire of thine head upon thee, and put on thy shoes upon thy feet, and cover not thy lips, and eat not the bread of men. So I spake unto the people in the morning: and at even my wife died; and I did in the morning as I was commanded.

—Ezekiel 24:15-18 KJV

It is a warm November again,
   and these windows in Michigan –
some glassed, some emptied –

collect me new caves
   of worn couches and broken blenders.
You prophesied, I guess,

a chariot, but I am still waiting for its fiery
   wheels to bear down on me.
I search for their charrings, I search for your

Rahab, and you wait for me
   in your tombing caves,
sipping from a trickling Chebar.

I pass one heretic or other
   in a waterless land called Babylon, but always find
myself back against a green-ish tree

in yet another Michigan winter – all browns,
   whites, greys, and this tree.
Who was your wife, the woman you swore

not to mourn? When did you know
    the people would stare at a pock-marked wall
receive spray after spray of paint

and offer the wall their GOLD?
    Where are the lakes that tried to recede
from the whole fleeing that is Detroit?

Where are the houses in Woodbridge?
    The ones that throw up cushionless couches
On porch after porch until the snow?

I am waiting for you.
    I am standing at the bottom
of a thirsting Rouge River,

the stillness wetting only my ankles.
    Even as it dries, this reddest river
refuses to ice.

How did you know the cities
    this world would try
to scrape empty?

Why could you not see
    what is here: these moments
of evaporation?

How Death Feeds Life
by Rick Lamplugh

One day early in February just after work, Mary and I start our dinner simmering and slip out of the bunkhouse kitchen and onto the back porch. Earlier today, one of the instructors stopped by the ranch to tell us that he had spotted a bison calf lying in the snow, and it didn't look well. He had watched it raise its head, try to stand up, and fall back down. The calf is across the main road from the ranch, close enough that from the back porch we should be able to see it with our naked eyes and zero in with a spotting scope.

I set up a scope, locate the calf, and zoom in on blood that dots the snow near its head, as if sprayed by a cough or sneeze. The instructor didn't know what had happened to the animal. I wonder if it has internal injuries after being hit by a visitor's car. The calf is so still that it looks dead, until the head rises a couple of inches and then flops back onto the snow.

There are no predators or scavengers nearby yet, but when I scan to the west, I discover a coyote mingling with a bison herd about a quarter mile away. Its head is down and its ears are twitching as it listens for a possible snack: mice or voles scurrying beneath the snow after being disturbed by the grazing bison. I step away from the scope so that Mary can take my place.

She swivels the scope and surveys the calf. "Huh," she mutters and zooms the instrument. A moment later she says, "I think I see coyote tracks. This could get interesting."

Mary and I are volunteers at the Lamar Buffalo Ranch in this remote northeastern corner of Yellowstone National Park. Throughout the winter we assist the visitors and instructors who come to the ranch for multi-day field seminars, often on wildlife watching. Though the Lamar River Valley is snow-covered most of the winter, it gets less snowfall than other areas of the park and draws winter-starved grazers, such as bison and elk. Wolves and coyotes follow prey. That confluence of wildlife against a white backdrop makes this small valley—it's just two miles wide and seven miles long—one of the best places in the world to watch the deadly dance between predator and prey.

Part of our job is to drive a fourteen-passenger bus full of eager seminar participants, wherever the instructor directs. We set up spotting scopes and help find wildlife. When not driving, we pull camp duty, shoveling snow from paths, and cleaning the bunkhouse, bathhouse, and thirteen visitor cabins. The workdays are long and full, but listening to a world-class tracker teach as I drive the bus or being serenaded by coyotes as I shovel snow can't be beat.

When Mary and I return to the kitchen, we dish up our dinner and sit at the dining room table with the two other volunteers, Karen and George. There are no seminars for a couple of days so the four of us have the bunkhouse to ourselves. I chatter on about how excited I am to watch what will happen to the calf. It could feed many other animals—could even draw a wolf pack. I want to observe and understand how the food chain develops, how death feeds life.

George says in a soft voice without taking his eyes off his soup, "I don't think it's right."

I stop a forkful of noodles halfway to my mouth and ask, "What's not right?"

"Watching the calf die," he says, staring at me.

"Why not?"

He sets his spoon down and rubs a hand over his head, which he shaved recently in support of his nephew, who lost his hair during chemotherapy. "It feels disrespectful to me. Like you're spying."

"Oh, come on, George. That calf will die whether I watch or not. And I doubt it knows I'm a quarter mile away and staring through a spotting scope."

He studies his bowl of soup and says, "I'd rather not hear any more about it."

There's a chilly silence until Karen changes the subject, and we finish eating in peace.

Peace is important. There are just six of us: four volunteers, the ranch manager, and a park ranger living and working all winter at the ranch. Though George has his cabin and Karen has hers, we volunteers eat and work together every day. Friction could make the winter very long.

Early the next morning, I return to the back porch alone and stand near the scope. I think about George's comments—and feel guilty. Was he right:

Am I a voyeur? I also wonder if the calf died overnight when the temperature fell to fifteen degrees. I can't imagine how it survived both the cold and its injury.

Curiosity starts to overcome guilt, and I scan with my naked eyes. A herd of about forty bison graze within a hundred yards of the calf but ignore it. I push away more guilt and peer into the scope. The calf is not moving. But a few moments later, the calf raises its head off the snow and then lays it back down.

I step from the scope and consider the situation. I'm not driving a bus today, so I'll be here cleaning. There is no field seminar and no participants are staying at the ranch. Mary will be in and out much of the day and everyone else will be gone. It's just me, this calf, and whatever is going to happen. This could be the first time I see who benefits from an animal's death and how they do so, the first time to try to take a naturalist's viewpoint. And that is a big part of why I wanted to volunteer in Yellowstone.

I first visited the park more than thirty years ago. I was a tourist, and Yellowstone was another spot to highlight in my dog-eared road atlas. Twenty-five years later, Mary and I returned and fell in love with this place. I was hooked and longed to learn more about this rare and fragile, wild and complete ecosystem.

More summers passed with more trips to bike, backpack, and canoe in Yellowstone. I learned something new every time and that whet my appetite for more. After we retired, Mary and I were accepted as winter volunteers. I arrived primed to immerse myself in this valley, to understand how its plants, animals, and geology fit together. This calf presents a perfect opportunity to do just that.

Regardless of George's objections and my conflicting feelings, I will scope this scene every hour or so and take notes with a digital voice recorder. But, for George's sake, I'll keep what I see to myself.

Two hours later I'm back at the scope with Mary. The calf has moved from one side of a willow bush to the other. Where the calf once lay, a couple of ravens waddle around, pecking at blood-stained snow. A big cow, probably the calf's mother, plods over from where she was grazing. She licks the calf's side; its body twitches and its head shakes. The few early-bird photographers, who have discovered this roadside photo opportunity, hunch over tripod-mounted cameras that sport expensive telephoto lenses.

Mary has her eye to a second scope and grumbles, "They're too close to that calf."

As I watch, a photographer with a lens as long as his arm and as big around as his head creeps even closer. "That lens is so powerful that he could just as easily back away and still get great shots," I say.

"Yeah, but he wants the money shot," Mary replies.

We have both spent numerous days driving groups of photographers in search of wildlife. We have heard them challenge each other about taking the "money shot," a picture so good that they can sell it or hang it proudly like a trophy.

An hour later I am back at the scope. The word is out; now fourteen photographers crowd the roadside in a feeding frenzy as the mom returns to the calf and nudges it with her big head. Though I can't hear from this distance, I bet she is making the low grunts that cows use to signal distress or locate a calf. With each nudge, the calf's body quivers, but the head doesn't move. Nine months ago, this calf walked and suckled within a few hours of birth. As it fed, its mother licked it, and her scent and touch filled the calf's new world. Now, as the calf slips from this world, that scent and touch must bring comfort again.

The mom swings her large head toward the road and stares in the direction of the photographers. Bison have poor vision; she probably can't see them, but she can hear and smell them. She turns back to the calf and nudges it again, careful not to poke it with her horns. The calf's mouth and nose are partially buried in the snow; breathing must be difficult.
The mom leaves and grazes a few yards away, head toward the photographers, aware of them. I chuckle as I imagine her charging and the photographers running for the protection of their cars. I widen the scope's field of vision to encircle mom and calf. Does she feel sad? Does the calf feel fear? I have read that once a bison cow senses she cannot save her calf—say, from an attacking grizzly—she will walk away. This is a matter of efficiency; half of all calves do not survive past their third winter. But a cow must save her energy to breed again; the herd's survival depends on it.

Still, no predators or scavengers are near the calf, other than the photographers who keep inching closer. As soon as one moves forward, another follows suit. I have found that photographers are like ravens: They'll find a kill anywhere. Ravens are so skilled at kill finding that some experts believe that hungry wolves travel to where they see ravens soaring and circling. Wolves would do well to watch photographers, too.

At lunchtime I leave my mop and bucket and return hesitantly to the bunkhouse and onto the back porch. I take a deep breath and look into the scope. The calf is so flat that it looks boneless. A single coyote, attentive and cautious, and judging from its size a male, stands about a yard from the calf's hindquarters. He skulks forward, sniffing, tail down. The calf twitches, and the coyote jumps back. A moment later he slinks closer, pokes the calf with his right front paw. The calf shudders, the coyote leaps back. This dance continues: The calf struggling to maintain its life, the coyote working to sustain his. The mom grazes a hundred yards away. Is she even aware of the danger to her calf?

The coyote moves in and ducks his head out of my view and into the tender—and vulnerable—underbelly near the calf's rear legs. When he comes back into view, he has a mouth full of fur. He dives back in and reappears with more fur. Eventually he's going to come up with hide and blood. Do I want to watch anymore?

I look around without the scope. There are at least twenty photographers now, the newest arrivals frantically erecting tripods in the road, right in the way of traffic. It hardly matters; visitors are stopping cars anywhere and everywhere; compelled to watch as the coyote stands atop the calf.

I also can't resist and turn back to the scope. The coyote looks like a dog with a pull toy: head low, canine teeth hooked into hide, front and rear legs stretched forward, back arched. While pulling, he repeatedly and violently twists his head from side to side. Even through the scope I can feel his power. The calf wriggles but cannot escape. The coyote is trying to eat the calf while it's still alive; once the animal dies, the meat will freeze. This meal will never be warmer, softer, or easier to eat. But understanding the efficiency of this doesn't make it any less gruesome to watch.

I step away from the scope, look down, and study the gray porch floor, its paint chipped here and there. I close my eyes, put a palm to each cheek, and shake my head. I open my eyes, look at the scope but not into it. I turn and stare at the door to the kitchen. Remembering my desire to see the food chain in action, I curse and step back to the scope.

No blood stains the coyote's muzzle, so he hasn't broken through yet. The calf raises its head and looks back at the predator. The coyote does not move away; he simply glances toward the calf's eyes and then at where he will bite next. The calf's head falls back to the snow, and a large cloud of breath, rises into the cold air, soft and white against the dark fur. I release a long, sad sigh.

The coyote circles the calf. He stares into the calf's eyes, and then saunters along the backbone to the rump. He pokes the calf, but it doesn't move. He pushes his muzzle against the calf. Still no movement. He yawns, looks almost bored. Perhaps he knows that the animal is dead and that there's no danger here, just a huge meal. There's no competition in sight, the sun is out, and the day is relatively warm—about 25 degrees. The coyote curls up in the snow.

I leave the scope; I don't need to watch this dog sleep. Instead, I go into the bunkhouse to have my lunch and escape the scene. Eating alone, I spend the mealtime lost in conflicting thoughts, feelings, and images about life, death, and watching an animal die.

After finishing a sandwich and convincing myself that observing how death feeds life is important, I return to the porch. The calf's mom is grazing a hundred yards away. Seventeen photographers zoom and focus and compose. The coyote is at the soft underbelly; his bloody muzzle shocks me. It took an hour, but he is finally in. I leave the porch, wondering if I'll continue watching now that blood has been drawn.

When I resume my watch later, the coyote is gone and so are most of the photographers. A raven sits in the snow far from the calf and appears to be eating. Possibly, while I was gone, the coyote ripped off a piece of meat and walked away with it, dropping scraps. As the calf gets spread around the landscape, the food chain will lengthen; scavengers—especially ravens— will feast.

Scientists have found that ravens are at a kill within minutes, sometimes even before the kill. Their beaks are not made for opening a carcass; they need coyotes—or wolves—to do that. They eat side-by-side with the dogs, often chased away but rarely harmed. They also fly off with bits of meat, cache this stash, and return for more. Scientists calculate that because of this caching, ravens actually get more meat from the kill than the wolves. Some believe that one reason wolves hunt in packs is so that they can consume more of a kill before ravens airlift it away.

Meat dangling from its beak, the raven flies off as a mating pair of coyotes approaches. I recognize these two; one a big male, the other a female with a tail ratty from mange. They have claimed this part of the valley as their territory. They stop and lie down in the snow some distance from the carcass. They are attentive to the photographers and show no sign of moving in on the meal.

When I next return to my vigil, a full day of observation has passed since I first spotted the calf. I lean against the kitchen doorframe and look across the road. A dozen photographers are still dining on the drama. Several are chatting like they're at a parade, voices drifting over to me on the breeze. The entire bison herd, with the mom on the fringe, is lying about seventy yards away from the carcass. While I'd like to think they are paying their respects, this is more likely what's called "loafing," a mundane step in their digestive process.

I hear the sound of coyotes yelping from Ranger Hill beside the bunkhouse. I wait for a reaction from the mating pair near the carcass. They throw their heads back; their breath escapes silently. Two seconds later their howls reach me. The Ranger Hill coyotes reply. I'm in the middle of a canine call and response. I smile and applaud silently.

When I return two hours later, only ravens and magpies are feeding. One raven sits on the head and pecks at the calf's eye. A bald eagle rests on a rock nearby, waiting its turn, though it dwarfs the other birds and could easily kill and eat them. One expert calls our national bird a shy scavenger, and from what I've seen, the name fits.

As the ravens dine, the single coyote that originally opened the carcass stands forty yards away, surveying them. He approaches cautiously, ears perked. The ravens and magpies depart; the eagle keeps its distance. The coyote sniffs around, pulls off a chunk of meat and drags it away, blood staining the snow.

I have no emotional reaction. I have stopped looking at the calf and seeing suffering. Now I look at a carcass and see sustenance. I've stopped viewing this as a conflicted tourist. Instead, I'm starting to analyze this as an objective naturalist.

When I next step onto the porch, Mary is again with me. The smell of pasta sauce follows us out the kitchen door, spices the air, and drifts away. Clouds have formed, the temperature has dropped, and snow is falling. Perhaps this is what chased away all the photographers, or maybe they're at dinner too. The bison herd is still far from the carcass, but two bison now bookend it. I can't tell if either is the mom.

I look into the scope and zoom in on the male coyote of the mating pair. He is eating and bloodied to his ears. He stops, walks away, and wipes either side of his face in the snow, painting bloody swaths. Then he rejoins his ratty-tailed mate. After some sniffing and snuggling, they return to the carcass and alternate short bursts of eating and peering into the fading daylight. A few moments later, the Ranger Hill coyotes yelp again, and I understand the pair's caution. I can't see the yelpers but can distinguish several voices.

Mary, watching through another scope pointed toward the yelping, whispers, "I think there's a wolf coming down the hill."

Two indistinct shapes move down the hill and in the direction of the bunkhouse. If they are wolves, they will run the coyotes off, but when they come closer, we can tell they are coyotes.

"I'll bet those are the ones we heard yelping a minute ago," I say.

"Raised leg urination!" Mary exclaims. The newcomer coyotes have raised a leg, urinated, and kicked snow on it. Only alphas—male and female—raise their legs to urinate, all other pack members squat. This alpha pair is marking territory already claimed by the other mating pair that's dining across the road. Trouble is brewing. The Ranger Hill coyotes move toward the road then back up the slope, and back to the road; an invisible line that separates them from a fight and a meal.

"Looks like they're trying to decide whether to challenge the other coyotes," I say, as a bull bison, huge in comparison, saunters right by the Ranger Hill coyotes.

As the Ranger Hill coyotes tussle with each other, Mary says, "I think they're egging each other on."

Finally, the newcomers cross the road and lope toward the carcass. The lope becomes a sprint. When they reach the mating pair, they slow down, lower their heads, bare their canines, tuck tails between their legs, and arch their backs.

"Alligator!" Mary yells, calling this dominance move by its coyote-watcher name.

One of the Ranger Hill coyotes chases the male of the mating pair. As they race away, the Ranger Hill coyote bites the male's rump. The male is the picture of fear: running full out, tail between his legs, mouth wide open, and head turned toward his pursuer.

Meanwhile, back at the carcass, the ratty-tailed female has strolled ten yards away and is nonchalantly washing her face and peacefully granting the carcass to the second Ranger Hill coyote.

Some of Yellowstone's wildlife biologists believe that because the Lamar

Valley is so small, and so full of wildlife, the animals that live here know one another. If this is true, it's possible that the Ranger Hill coyotes knew that the male of the mating pair wouldn't leave without a squabble. And that his mate was not real competition and could be allowed to stroll.

The Ranger Hill coyote stops the chase and trots back to the carcass, head high. He joins his partner in their prize. The vanquished male sits and cleans himself.

I move the scope around and spot the single coyote that discovered and opened the calf. From a safe distance, he is watching the two pairs battle. All five coyotes look healthy. This fits what a wolf watcher told me: Since wolf reintroduction in 1995, only smart and strong coyotes have survived.

The last sight I see before darkness draws a curtain across the scene is the Ranger Hill coyotes ravaging the carcass. Mary and I also head into dinner. I long to describe to George and Karen the turf battle and alligators we just witnessed. I want to share my detailed observations of who ate what, but I keep my mouth shut.

During the night, through our open cabin window, Mary and I hear more coyote howling than we have all winter. In the dark, we whisper and wonder if this is due to the carcass and a turf war.

Early the next morning the resident ranger, Brian, moves the carcass another quarter mile from the road to reduce the roadside danger created by the pack of photographers. The photographers, so focused on shooting, could easily step into the road and be hit by the car of a driver, who is just as distracted.

Brian stops by the bunkhouse and says that the calf was born nine months ago. It would have been gaining about forty pounds a month and probably weighs more than three hundred pounds. That's a nice meal for five coyotes, a flock of ravens, some magpies, and a shy bald eagle.

Two days after I started observing the calf, I step to the scope and study the remains: ribs and backbone, bright red and stripped of meat. The hide lies on the snow, a rumpled rug. I count fifteen ravens, some calling to each other, and three magpies. Two coyotes stand at opposite ends of the remains, until one runs the other off with the alligator move. Only two photographers brave the cold wind blowing in from the southwest. The rest of their pack has moved on, hungry for other shots.

Later, just after dinner, when I check the scope for the last time, the only creature left is a single magpie. I walk away from the scope, down the steps, and along the ranch's snow-covered driveway that winds toward the main road. Each step away from the scope relieves me.

Though we've backpacked for years deep in Yellowstone's backcountry, I've had a tourist's view of wildlife framed by spectacular scenery. I've detoured around bison, run from a charging moose family, and backed down from an ornery elk. I've marveled at a racing antelope, watched a coyote walk right through a line of spectators, and been spellbound by a wolf pack trotting along a sunlit ridge.

Until now I have never forced myself to watch the bloody death and life battle as prey fights death and predator struggles to survive. I have never observed from a naturalist's point of view, never witnessed firsthand how death feeds life. The part of me that loves these animals is glad that this first time is over. But another part—the naturalist, who doesn't want to just love, but wants to understand what he loves—hopes that it's not the last.

Eastern Oregon Triptych
by Donald Wolff

I

As I drive a hundred miles to the next state to see a heart specialist, I can easily take in the wide empty spaces of eastern Oregon, where today even the long rolling hills green with six-inch tall spring wheat seem impermanent.

II

On the way to Ontario, just outside of La Grande, I saw a coyote standing straight and tall in the middle of a small fenced-in herd of cattle. The cows seemed oblivious, grazing in a scattered circle around it. The calves stayed near their mothers, whose bulk perplexed the coyote thinking about what to do next, frozen by hunger, need, and the odds against him.

III

How far I've come to write this. The Imnaha running steady and clear on a lucent day, while I sit next to it in my blue camping chair. Nearby the water eddies while these words from my fountain pen lay peeled blue black on paper bright with the sun. The white water is wide here, the white noise drowning out the empty phrases, the failure of words.

Don't Forget
by Ada Molinoff

Poets (8)   [card for Eleanor's July 6th birthday]
lem wedges
Salmon salad
crackers
cheeses
cut up melon
dates? (Lois might bring)
ice tea
glasses
choc chip cake

Rosh Hashanah lunch (8)
lox   *glass leaf dish?*
onion slices, capers   *blue plate*
3 cheeses, incl neuchatel   *wh sm plate*
breads / pita / round challah fr. Cascade Baking   *basket*
crackers   *small basket*
appetizers – hummus (Marney)
                 carrots
                 cherry toms
tabouli (Marilyn)
Kugel, as dessert   *glass oblong dish*

teas / *mugs*
apples & honey (Millie)
nuts (Alice)   *Italian dish & spn*
        Remember Alice's 90th birthday

Poets (8) [for Virginia's 1/31 birthday]
        [Dina—flowering plant]
tea water

teas

mugs

cranberry sparkling juice—V.'s fave—

   & glasses

forks

naps

caviar pie, lem wedges

crisps, crackers

plates for pumpkin cake

Note on calendar Virginia's surgery, 2/4

For Rosh Hashanah (8? 7? Alice strong enough?)

Kugel, as main dish

   buy noodles, cottage cheese, sour cream

   count eggs

   check butter, cinnamon

   golden raisins still good?

lox etc.

green salad (who?)

teas

9/30

Freeze leftover Kugel

Note on recipe: Carolyn is gluten-free

Marilyn—no dairy

Sherry—no cinnamon

Poets (8) [gifts for Stephanie's girls]

Unfreeze Kugel

Poets (7)

Tea & H2O / mugs

2 cheeses

2 crackers

Galette

include crans, in memory of our Virginia, with pears, cinn,
ape jam, & pecans?

10/21
Write Colette's suggestion on recipe—
galette under broiler
to crisp crust
and meld flavors
at end

Contributors

Judith Arcana writes poems, stories and essays. Her recent collections are poetry: *The Parachute Jump Effect*, *4th Period English*, and *What If Your Mother*. One of her stories is out as a zine (*Keesha and Joanie and JANE*); two related pieces are online at *Serving House Journal*. She's now completing the Maude poems, a project supported by grants from The Celebration Foundation and NW Oregon's Regional Arts and Culture Council. In 2013, a sandwich was named for her at Fleur de Lis, a really good bakery/cafe in Portland. Listen to Judith on SoundCloud; visit juditharcana.com.

Kaitlyn Burch is a recent graduate from Portland State's MFA program. Previously her stories have appeared in *VoiceCatcher* and *The Portland Review*. Besides writing, she teaches dance to middle school and high schoolers in the Portland area.

John Byrne lives in Albany, Oregon with his wife, Cheryl, an artist, and their writer/actress high school aged daughter. He writes short stories, plays and poems. Some of his work appeared in the first two issues of *Gold Man Review*. Other writing can be found in *The Lyric*, *Fiction Vortex*, *Chamber Four*, and other print and internet journals. *Passage Money* was triggered by childhood memories of living in eastern Long Island and listening to the radio report the sinking of the Andrea Doria.

Michael Coolen taught in the Music Department at Oregon State University for 32 years, retiring 3 years ago, by intention, on April Fools Day. He has lived and worked in Africa, New Zealand, France, and Denmark.

Julia Kolchinsky Dasbach came to the United States as a Jewish refugee in 1993, from Dnepropetrovsk, Ukraine. She holds an MFA in Poetry from the University of Oregon and is a Ph.D. candidate in Comparative Literature at the University of Pennsylvania. Julia's honors include *Lilith Magazine's* 2013 Charlotte A. Newberger Poetry Prize and the 2011 Karen

Jackson Ford Poetry Prize, among others. Her work has appeared in or is forthcoming from *Spoon River Poetry Review*, *Guernica*, *JMWW*, *Cirque*, and various other journals. Julia is also the Poetry Editor for *Construction Magazine*.

Ken Embery, born and raised in the Pacific Northwest, has had a lifelong love of writing. As a graduate student, commercial video director, television reporter, and Executive Producer in the video game business, he found many ways to earn a living with writing. But the screenplays, news stories, and non-fiction he wrote always felt artificial. It took the death of his wife, Julie, and the subsequent discovery of body-surfing in Maui, to remind him of Sandburg and Bly, Lawrence and Bukowski, Kinnell and Cummings. Mr. Embery believes there is unique truth in poetry; truth distilled through the love of life, family, and universal moments; truth made musical by the rhythm of words.

Linda Ferguson's fiction, poetry, and essays have appeared in journals such as *Perceptions*, *Saranac Review*, *Square Lake*, *Pure Francis*, and *Fiction at Work*. She lives in Portland, Oregon, where she teaches creative writing and dance.

K. F. Hanson is a mature writer who has enjoyed many years of public service in Oregon. As to her background: she was conceived in Manhattan, born in Idaho, and raised in rural Oregon; all of which have given her a deep appreciation for kosher hot dogs, the Metropolitan Museum of Art, ghost towns, crawdad catching, and mint farms. Many of her waking hours as a child were spent roaming the fields and riverbanks of the Northwest and finding comfort in its care. To her, then as now, this piece of earth, the soil itself, is ever capable of redeeming and transforming us all. It is that sense she hopes to convey in her writing. Previous published work is limited to a single poem printed in a hometown newspaper at age thirteen. She is currently working on a novel about the will to believe and the lies that are sometimes required.

Donna Henderson is the author of three collections of poems, most recently her 2009 collection *The Eddy Fence*. Her collections have twice been finalists for the Oregon Book Award in poetry. She is the founding editor of Airlie Press and a licensed clinical social worker. Donna maintains a psychotherapy practice in Monmouth, Oregon, and teaches both counseling and creative writing at area colleges. She holds an MSW from Portland State University and an MFA from Warren Wilson College.

Nazifa Islam grew up in Novi, Michigan. Her poetry and paintings have appeared in *Anomalous Press, Splinterswerve, The Fat City Review*, and *Flashquake* among many others, and her debut poetry collection *Searching for a Pulse* (2013) was released by Whitepoint Press. She sometimes updates her blog, "Thoughts Interjected," and can be found on Twitter at @nafoopal. She is currently pursuing a Master of Fine Arts in poetry at Oregon State University.

Marc Janssen had the pleasure to be published in the first and second *Gold Man Review* editions and participate in a number of readings. In addition to this publication, in the last few months he also had work appear in *Ottawa Arts Review, Vine Leaves Literary Journal*, and *Dead Flowers: A Poetry Rag* as well as in the anthology *The Color of Winter is Green*.

Marilyn Johnston is a Salem writer and filmmaker. She received a Robert Penn Warren Award and an Oregon Literary Arts Fellowship. Her work has appeared in *Calyx, Windfall*, and *To Topos Poetry International*, among others. Poems from *Red Dust Rising*, her chapbook about a family's recovery from war, were nominated for a Pushcart Prize.

Chelsea R. G. Kachman is pursuing an MFA and MA at Portland State University in Portland, OR. Her work has appeared or is forthcoming in *Drunken Boat, The Portland Review, Emerge Literary Journal*, and others.

Kelly Kittel has spent most of her working life as a fish biologist who writes but is undergoing a metamorphosis to a writer who used to be a fish biologist. She has handled fish for most of her life, from bass fishing as a kid in Maine to sexing pollock onboard a Japanese mothership in the Bering Sea to saving the salmon in the Pacific Northwest. She and her family divide their time between a house on an island in Rhode Island and a yurt on the coast of Oregon. She has been published in a number of anthologies and magazines, most recently in *41N* with articles on both scallops and quahogs. She writes a blog entitled "Where in the World are the Kittels?" and her memoir, *Breathe*, is scheduled to be published May 2014 by SheWrites Press.

Don Kunz taught literature, creative writing, and film studies at the University of Rhode Island for 36 years and is an Emeritus Professor of English now retired to Bend, Oregon where he continues to write for publication, volunteer in the SMART Reader Program and Family Kitchen (which feeds the hungry), play Native American Flute, and study Spanish.

Rick Lamplugh has been writing literary nonfiction for the last five years. His current project is a book, *In the Temple of Wolves*, about living and working in Yellowstone National Park during the winter. He has submitted stand-alone chapters from that book-in-progress to literary contests and journals. One story won the 2012 Jim Stone Non-Fiction award. Another placed in two contests, one national and one international. A third appeared in *Composite Arts Magazine*. A fourth was published on the blog of "Coyote Watch Canada." Some of those stories are on his blog, "Yellowstone Stories and Images." http://www.ricklamplugh.blogspot.com/

Laura LeHew has won state and national awards including residencies from Soapstone and MAR. Her poems appear in *Eleven Eleven, FutureCycle: American Society: What Poet's See, PANK, Slice and Spillway a Poetry Magazine*. Collections: *Beauty* (Tiger's Eye Press), *It's Always Night, It Always Rains* (Winterhawk Press) and forthcoming *Willingly Would I Burn* (MoonPath Press). Laura received her MFA from CCA. Former president of the Oregon Poetry Association she recently joined the board of *Calyx*, www.calyxpress.org. Laura writes, edits her small press Uttered Chaos and sharpens her claws in Eugene, Oregon—www.utteredchaos.org.

Amy Miller has work that has appeared in *Northwest Review, Nimrod, Bellingham Review, Many Mountains Moving, Gold Man Review, ZYZZYVA*, and other journals. Her eight chapbooks of poetry and essays include *Tea Before Questions, The Mechanics of the Rescue*, and *Fred Meyer, Mi Amore*. She lives in Ashland, where she works as the publications manager for the Oregon Shakespeare Festival.

Ada Molinoff's poems have appeared in literary journals, anthologies, and newspapers. "Don't Forget" memorializes Virginia Corrie-Cozart—poet, watercolorist, and friend. Ada earned her MFA in Nonfiction from Pacific University, having entered the program in poetry. She writes in both genres from Salem, Oregon.

Mike Newman is an artist, writer, and teacher living in The Dalles, Oregon. He plans to retire from teaching in one year and devote his time to reading, writing, and painting.

Paulann Petersen, Oregon's sixth Poet Laureate, has six full-length books of poetry, most recently *Understory* from Lost Horse Press in 2013. Her poems have appeared in many journals and anthologies, including *Poetry*, *The New Republic*, *Prairie Schooner*, *Willow Springs*, *Calyx*, and the Internet's *Poetry Daily*. She was a Stegner Fellow at Stanford University and the recipient of the 2006 Holbrook Award from Oregon Literary Arts. She serves on the board of Friends of William Stafford, organizing the January Stafford Birthday Events.

Eileen Pettycrew was raised on a cotton and potato farm in California's San Joaquin Valley, but has been an Oregon resident for many years. After earning degrees in chemistry, Eileen worked in quality control and teaching before turning to writing and editing while raising two daughters. Her book, *Growing Up Girl*, was published in 2003 by Saint Mary's Press. Eileen works at the University of Portland and lives in southeast Portland with her husband, Jim.

Jean Rover is a Salem, Oregon writer with an extensive background in corporate and marketing communications. She now writes fiction, poetry and personal essays. More recently, her work has appeared in *Gold Man Review*, *Work Literary Magazine*, *Rose Red Review*, the *This I Believe* project and various periodicals. Her novel, *Touch the Sky*, is looking for a publisher. Jean is a member of Willamette Writers and Oregon Writers Colony. She is an award-winning business communicator.

Tim Schell is the winner of the 2004 Mammoth Book Award for Prose for his novel *The Drums of Africa*, which was published in the fall of 2007. In 2010, Tim's novel *The Memoir of Jake Weedsong* was the Finalist in the AWP novel competition, and in 2011 it was published by Serving House Books.

Tim's fiction has been nominated for a Pushcart Award and he was the winner of the Martindale Award for Long Fiction. A section of his novel *Road to the Sea*, Finalist in the 1995 AWP novel competition, appears in the Fall 2006 issue of *Ploughshares*. Tim is the Chair of the Writing, Literature and Foreign Language Department at Columbia Gorge Community College.

Penelope Schott's recent chapbook is *Lovesong For Dufur*. The new full-length collection of poems on prostitution is called *Lillie Was A Goddess, Lillie Was A Whore*. She lives in Portland and sometimes in Dufur, Oregon.

Jennifer Springsteen has been published in numerous literary magazines and been lucky enough to receive two Pushcart nominations. She received an Oregon Literary Arts Fellowship in 2008, which jump started all of the work she has published since then. She has compiled many of her stories into a collection that she hopes to publish in the next year, and is currently at work on a novel. Jennifer and the co-founder of PDX Writers are facilitating workshops in the Portland area and she is working as an editor and coach for writers from all over.

Geronimo Tagatac has published fiction in *Orion Magazine*, *The Northwest Review*, *Phantom Drift*, and other journals. He has published stories in anthologies, including *Tilting the Continent* and *Growing Up Filipino II*. *The Weight of the Sun*, his collection of short stories, was nominated for the Oregon Book Award, in 2007.

Cristina White writes poetry and plays, fiction and creative non-fiction. Her essays and poetry have appeared in *Orion Magazine*, *The Spirit of Corvallis*, and *VoiceCatcher*; her published work includes a children's play, *The Enchanted Journey* (Samuel French) and a book, *The Healing Environment* (Celestial Arts). Two recent short plays have been staged in Corvallis and Newport. She is an avid line dancer, loves to walk, and does Tai Chi daily, a discipline she taught for many years in Los Angeles and the San Francisco Bay Area. She and her life partner live in Corvallis, where they tend a pocket garden.

Donald Wolff's poems have appeared in numerous magazines and anthologies. *Soon Enough*, a book length collection of poems, was published by Wordcraft in 2007. He is currently completing his second collection, *What's*

Close to Me.

Matt Young writes short fiction. He's been published a few times, most notably in the *Gold Man Review* out of Salem, Oregon and *Midwestern Gothic* out of Ann Arbor, Michigan. Mainly, he receives rejection letters, which while semi-heartbreaking, give him the slightest glimmer of hope, because it means someone actually read what he wrote and felt something about it—even if it was a negative feeling. While Oregon is home, he and his wife, Jenna currently live with their overly energetic dog and runty cat in Oxford, Ohio, where Matt is pursuing his MA in creative writing at Miami University.